FIRST BLOOD
IN NORTH AFRICA

FIRST BLOOD IN NORTH AFRICA

Operation Torch and the U.S. Campaign in Africa in WWII

Jon Diamond

STACKPOLE BOOKS

Guilford, Connecticut

Published by Stackpole Books
An imprint of Globe Pequot

Distributed by
NATIONAL BOOK NETWORK

British Library Cataloguing in Publication Information available

Library of Congress Cataloging-in-Publication Data

Names: Diamond, Jon (Jonathan Russell), author.
Title: First blood in North Africa : Operation Torch and the U.S. campaign in
    Africa in WWII / Jon Diamond.
Description: Lanham, Maryland : Stackpole Books, an imprint of Globe Pequot,
    trade division of the Rowman & Littlefield Publishing Group, Inc., 2017. |
    Includes bibliographical references.
Identifiers: LCCN 2016033734 (print) | LCCN 2016034537 (ebook) | ISBN
    9780811717779 (pbk.) | ISBN 780811765619 (e-book) | ISBN 9780811765619
    (ebook)
Subjects: LCSH: World War, 1939-1945—Campaigns—Africa, North. | Operation
    Torch, 1942. | Africa, North—History, Military.
Classification: LCC D766.82 .D53 2017 (print) | LCC D766.82 (ebook) | DDC
    940.54/231—dc23
LC record available at https://lccn.loc.gov/2016033734

Printed in the United States of America

CONTENTS

CHAPTER 1
STRATEGIC OVERVIEW AND THE WAR IN NORTH AFRICA, 1940–1942

The interval from October 1942 through January 1943 has been referred to as a "turning of the tide" in the epic struggle of World War II. During this three-month time frame, five major land campaigns were conducted, leading to staggering losses for the Axis partners of Germany and Italy as well as the Japanese Empire. These included the protracted battles for Papua New Guinea; Guadalcanal, in the southern Solomon Islands of the South Pacific Area; across the Western Desert of the North African littoral, culminating in the First and Second Battles of El Alamein; the defense of Stalingrad, resulting in the surrender of large numbers of Axis coalition troops, comprising mostly the *Wehrmacht*'s Sixth Army; and the invasion of Northwest Africa on November 8, 1942, Operation Torch.

First, in the Southwest Pacific Area, after the Japanese withdrew from their overland assault on Port Moresby, New Guinea, Gen. Douglas A. MacArthur's American and Australian forces captured the Japanese garrisons at Buna and Gona on the northern coast of Papua New Guinea, albeit at horrific cost to those troops fighting in that hellacious locale. The victory over the tenacious Japanese defenders at Buna and Gona, along with a previous repulsion of an enemy amphibious assault at Milne Bay in late August and early September 1942, effectively ensured that Port Moresby would not be attacked again from the eastern half of New Guinea.

Second, in the South Pacific, the U.S. Marine Corps' 1st Division (Reinforced), along with U.S. Army contingents initially from the Americal (23rd) Infantry Division, held off repeated Japanese land, sea, and air assaults to continue to maintain control over Henderson Field on the northern plain of the southern Solomon Island, Guadalcanal. Eventually more-substantial American forces went on the offensive, causing the Japanese to completely withdraw from Guadalcanal by the end of the first week of February 1943.

Third, at Stalingrad, Soviet forces made an epic defense within that city's streets against the *Wehrmacht*'s Gen. Friedrich von Paulus and his vaunted Sixth Army, some of the finest troops in the German army. The planning for Operation Torch would have

been for naught had the Germans won their epic clash with the Soviets. By October 1942 two Nazi armies had driven forward deep into the Soviet interior's Caucasus Mountains but had become bogged down only a few miles from the oil fields that Hitler required to continue his war effort. Just to the north of the Caucasus Mountains was the city of Stalingrad on the Volga River. It was to become the farthest point that the German Sixth Army and 4th Panzer Army would advance to. On October 2 von Paulus unleashed his last offensive against the Russians in Stalingrad, namely, a 2,000-yard deep pocket, which included the gutted remains of buildings and factories. The German gains were measured in yards, and von Paulus admitted to his peers, "Things are going very slowly, but every day we make a little progress. The whole thing is a question of time and manpower." The *Wehrmacht* could not do anything to delay winter's onset, nor could they tap into any ready reinforcements for von Paulus's dwindling Sixth Army ranks. The German High Command knew that if Stalingrad was not captured within a month, the whole Nazi position in southern Russia would be a precarious one since their flanks to the north and west were held by Rumanian troops. As it happened, the flanks were overrun by a Russian winter counteroffensive, and despite Gen. Erich von Manstein's attempt to open a corridor to von Paulus's troops, the Sixth Army was encircled and forced to surrender. The loss of the Sixth Army's twenty divisions doomed the German invasion of the Soviet Union.

Fourth, British prime minister Winston S. Churchill and his chief of the Imperial General Staff (CIGS), Gen. Sir Alan Brooke, needed to engage the Axis forces somewhere; however, both were dreadfully afraid of sending another expeditionary force to the European continent or Scandinavia after the disasters at Dunkirk and Norway in the spring of 1940. In the future both British leaders would also learn that an attack on a fortified continental port was suicidal, as evidenced at Dieppe during Operation Jubilee in August 1942, which inflicted horrific casualties on the assaulting Canadian infantry and British armor. An understanding of the campaign in Northwest Africa requires a description of the combat events that occurred in the Western Desert of Egypt and Libya from December 9, 1940, through November 8, 1942, the latter date corresponding to the Operation Torch landings in French Morocco and Algeria.

The Italian Fascist dictator, Benito Mussolini, gave the British War Cabinet its entrée into a land battle against the junior Axis partner across the North African littoral and in rugged and remote East Africa, rather than on the European continent. On June 11, 1940, as the French were about to capitulate, Mussolini declared war on Britain and France. Soon thereafter, in the late summer of 1940, Italy's Tenth Army under Gen. Rodolfo Graziani launched its laborious advance across the frontier from Cyrenaican Libya into Egypt. This would later develop into a full-scale theater of war, which pitted British and Commonwealth forces against the Axis fascist partners. Initially Gen. Archibald Wavell, commander in chief (C-in-C), Middle East, decided that he had to attack and rid this threat against his western flank by the Italian presence with a "short and swift operation, lasting from four to five days at the most, and taking every advantage of the element of surprise" in the Sofafi–Sidi Barrani–Buqbuq area. The British C-in-C faced 215,000 Italians with only 36,000 of his own forces. Wavell, after detailed clandestine planning, sent a relatively small combined infantry, the 4th Indian Division, and armored contingent, the 7th Royal Tank Regiment (RTR) with their heavy Infantry tanks nicknamed "Matildas." This combined British and Indian unit, initially called the Western Desert Force, was under the command of Lt. Gen. Sir Richard O'Connor. Its orders were to conduct a "limited raid": from December 9–11, 1940, to evict those elements of Mussolini's Italian Tenth Army from their fortified Egyptian desert camps at Nibeiwa as well as at Tummar East and West. In addition, O'Connor's Western Desert Force would then proceed to capture the port town of Sidi Barrani. In all, a total of 20,000 Italians surrendered and 180 artillery guns and 60 tanks were seized as thousands more streamed westward in a pell-mell fashion across the coastal road toward Italy's other port garrisons.

Having replaced the 4th Indian Division, now bound to fight the Italians in Eritrea, Australian troops in the Australian Imperial Force's (AIF) 6th Division, after acclimatization and desert training in Palestine and Egypt, captured Bardia on January 5, 1941. There the "haul" was 38,000 Italian prisoners along with numerous coastal guns, field guns, antiaircraft (AA) pieces, and vehicles. The

British secretary for war, Anthony Eden, sardonically quipped, "never has so much been surrendered by so many to so few." On January 1 the Western Desert Force was renamed XIII Corps and Wavell set his eyes on Benghazi; however, Churchill was already siphoning off some of XIII Corps and Royal Air Force (RAF) elements for an inopportune expedition against the Axis partners in Greece.

Nonetheless, O'Connor had received permission to continue his "raid" as far west as Benghazi once Tobruk was captured from the Italians. Tobruk was assaulted by the Australian 6th Division and fell on January 22, 1941. More than 25,000 Italian prisoners were taken, along with hundreds of field guns. Again, the Italians were in full retreat to the west of Tobruk. After capturing Derna on January 30, 1941, O'Connor decided to maintain his pursuit of the Italians along the coast with the intent of destroying the entire enemy Tenth Army. His plan was to have the British 7th Armoured Division move swiftly to the southwest in order to cut the road below Benghazi and trap the retreating Italians in the Cyrenaican "bulge" with a double envelopment. One arm of his Corps reached Sidi Saleh, 10 miles south of Beda Fomm, on February 5, blocking the retreat of the remnants of the entire Italian Tenth Army into Libya's Tripolitania half. Fighting raged for almost two days, until the Italians surrendered late on February 7. An additional 20,000 Italians were captured, along with more than 100 tanks and field guns.

O'Connor signaled Wavell, "Fox killed in open," and he believed that after capturing Benghazi he would receive orders from him to press the attack to Tripoli. However, Wavell had ended any hope of XIII Corps being sent to Tripoli, since on February 10 the War Cabinet had ruled out continuing any possibility of continuing the advance. Wavell was instructed to give first and foremost priority to assisting Greece, which he had grave misgivings about since a continued advance through Libya would result in the capture of the port of Tripoli and finally evict the Italian Fascist forces from North Africa entirely. So, after conquering the Cyrenaican half of Libya's North African littoral and freeing the Egyptian frontier from the Italian invader, XIII Corps went onto the defensive at El Agheila at the base of the Gulf of Sirte, but only for a brief spell. Tragically, the Greek venture became a disaster for Wavell, ultimately leading to a forced Allied evacuation from the Peloponnese and the subsequent loss of Crete to a German airborne invasion in the late spring of 1941.

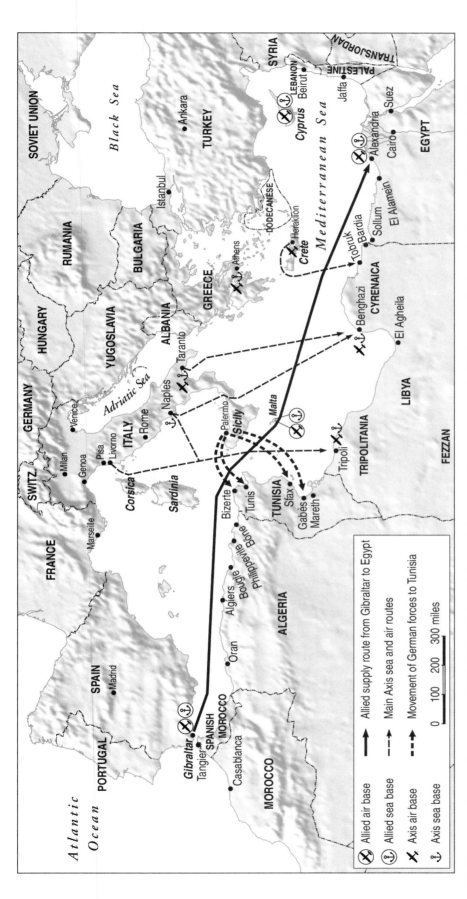

Mediterranean theater of operations, 1940–1943. Allied and Axis supply lines, stretching across the entire Mediterranean basin, for the disparate and myriad battlefields of the Middle East and North African littoral. A complete rout of the Italian Tenth Army and capture of their principal port garrisons at Bardia, Tobruk, and Benghazi was achieved by British and Allied forces, comprising the Western Desert Force (later designated British XIII Corps), during Gen. Archibald Wavell's Operation Compass from early December 1940 to early February 1941. Following that much desired victory for Britain and her dominions against Mussolini's Fascist troops, a "seesaw" set of desert engagements, including the siege, relief, and ultimate Axis capture of Tobruk, was waged across the Cyrenaican half of Libya from El Agheila through the Egyptian frontier to El Alamein from late February 1941 to November 1942. The combatants were now strongly mechanized Axis forces, striking from Tripoli under the battlefield leadership of *Deutsches Afrikakorps* (DAK) commander Gen. Erwin Rommel, and a reinforced and more powerfully armed multinational British Eighth Army, led successively by Generals Claude Auchinleck and Bernard Montgomery. The British Eighth Army's victory over Rommel's *Panzer-Armee Afrika* at El Alamein in late October to mid-November 1942 served as a strategic prelude for Operation Torch and its principal amphibious landings across Northwest Africa at Casablanca, Oran, and Algiers on November 8, 1942. The Torch landings and capitulation of Vichy French forces in Morocco and Algeria would serve as the beginning of a six-month campaign of bitter combat throughout Tunisia between steadily reinforced Allied forces through the three above-mentioned ports and a newly created Axis force, the 5th Panzer Army, built up in Tunis and Bizerte and composed of German and Italian troops, under the command of Gen. Hans-Jürgen von Arnim. The westward retreat of Rommel's *Panzer-Armee Afrika* with the pursuit by Montgomery's Eighth Army across the Tripolitanian portion of Italian-controlled Libya would add to the conflict in southern Tunisia during the initial months of 1943 until final victory over the Axis in North Africa in May 1943. MERIDIAN MAPPING

In early 1941 Hitler's original plan to bolster the Italians after the defeat at Beda Fomm was to provide German antitank (AT), AA, and armored units. Initially a motorized light division (5th Light Division) and the 15th Panzer Division were ordered to Libya in early 1941, under the command of *Generalleutnant* Erwin Rommel. This force would comprise the initial nucleus of the *Wehrmacht*'s vaunted *Deutsches Afrikakorps* (DAK). On February 12 Rommel arrived in Tripoli and exceeded his orders by assuming control of the German forward area and ordered his newly arriving armored units east toward the British. Rather than waiting for reinforcements, Rommel sent his reconnaissance units forward to bluff the British into believing he had superior strength. At this stage of the desert war, the British now had inferior armor and AT weapons compared to their newly arrived German adversaries. During the last week of March, the fledgling units that were to become the DAK attacked and captured the British defensive position at Mersa Brega. After Rommel pressed onto Agedabia, O'Connor, who was back at Egyptian headquarters, was ordered to join British general Sir Philip Neame and the remnants of XIII Corps at the front. Rommel's intent was to cut the Cyrenaican bulge, the reverse of what O'Connor had achieved only weeks before, with his initial objectives being Derna and then Tobruk. Other DAK forces were dispatched along the coast road, and Benghazi was recaptured by the Axis on April 4. General Neame ordered a complete withdrawal eastward. On April 6 the 9th Australian Division withdrew from Derna into Tobruk. Wavell recognized that Tobruk was the linchpin in the region, and he reinforced the major port with another Australian brigade from the 7th Australian Division. Other brigades from this division went to Mersa Matruh in Egypt to shore up defenses there. While Rommel invested Tobruk for a lengthy and historic siege, Wavell was also concerned about maintaining Egypt as Britain's base in the Middle East. During the early hours of April 7, Generals Neame and O'Connor were both captured by the Germans as they tried to get back to the British lines during the retreat. By April 14 Rommel had cleared all of Cyrenaica except for the Australian units garrisoning Tobruk, who were holed up like "desert rats" for a developing siege. Rommel's eastward advance on Egypt was halted at Halfaya Pass, because here Wavell reacquired shorter lines of communication, while Rommel, without the port facilities of Tobruk, had long supply lines to the rear with limited reinforcements.

On May 1, as Rommel attacked Tobruk, Wavell began to plan an offensive, Operation Battleaxe, once armored reinforcements, Churchill's "Tiger" Convoy, arrived later in the month. However, before the new tanks were even off-loaded, Wavell acted on intelligence received that Rommel had limited armor along the Egyptian frontier. So the British commander attacked the Germans by sending all of the remaining British tanks in the Western Desert along with the support group of the 7th Armoured Division to attack on May 15, Operation Brevity, in which he tried to recapture Halfaya Pass. Initially the attack was successful, but within a fortnight the DAK counterattacked and took it back again. Wavell tried again on June 15 with the more ambitious Battleaxe planning and new tanks; however, the results were similar, as Rommel employed his 88mm AT/AA guns in a defensive role, as he had at Arras in France in 1940 against the heavy British I (Matilda) tanks there. On June 17 the British force returned to Sidi Barrani, while Wavell withdrew the 7th Armoured Division to Mersa Matruh to refit, leaving mobile reconnaissance forces to keep Rommel at bay. The British had lost more than 150 tanks. Wavell had been defeated in a series of battles since the high watermark of his tenure at Beda Fomm in February 1941, but Rommel was stagnant since reinforcements were diverted to the *Wehrmacht*'s invasion of the Soviet Union on June 22, 1941, Operation Barbarossa. Moreover, Tobruk remained in Allied possession, but Churchill had lost confidence in Wavell as his newly reinforced armored force had been decimated convincingly by Rommel's DAK.

On June 22, 1941, Wavell received his dismissal, and Churchill wanted him to exchange places with Gen. Sir Claude Auchinleck, C-in-C India. During the summer of 1941, XIII Corps was reinforced by the addition of XXX Corps and became the Eighth Army under the command of Lt. Gen. Sir Alan Cunningham, who commanded the southern wing of Wavell's pincer based in Kenya that conquered Italian Somaliland and then Ethiopia. Lieutenant General Cunningham, the brother of the British admiral Andrew Cunningham, would lead a new, larger offensive, Operation Crusader, which was to outflank the German defensive positions at Halfaya and then relieve the Tobruk garrison. This attack began on November 18, 1941, and was to coincide with an attempted breakout of the Tobruk garrison to link up with the Eighth Army. Cunningham's XXX Corps did outflank the German defenses at Halfaya Pass and broke out into the open desert, but at Sidi Rezegh, Rommel's forces dealt a sharp blow to the inferior British armor and destroyed the bulk of XXX Corps' tanks. Seeing a chance to get behind XXX, Rommel chose to attack eastward and cut the British forces from their base. While Cunningham urged a retreat, a resolute Auchinleck, who had been valiant during the Norwegian debacle in 1940 as well as leading admirably in the defense of the oil fields of Iraq, ordered all of his units to attack the enemy wherever they were and then pursue them. Lt. Gen. Neil Ritchie replaced a war-weary Cunningham, and Rommel suffered from having to fight the British in the east and confront the Allied garrison at Tobruk in his rear. It was really Auchinleck who directed the resumption of the British attack on Sidi Rezegh, which unbalanced Rommel, enabling Ritchie to move on to Tobruk to lift the siege, after a last-ditch effort by the DAK to take Tobruk failed on December 5, 1941. The following day Rommel retreated westward, with the British pursuing him to a line of El Agheila-Marada, which was the German starting point in March 1941. Rommel dug in there and awaited reinforcements.

On January 5, 1942, Rommel was reinforced with tanks, armored cars, AT and AA guns, and notably the 90th Light Division. On the other hand, Auchinleck's position had been weakened by the removal of British and Australian formations to the Far East to counter Japan's blitzkrieg throughout the Pacific Rim and beyond. Rommel completely surprised both Auchinleck and the British Eighth Army by attacking them from his defenses at El Agheila on January 21, and if not for a speedy withdrawal by the Allies, they would have been completely overrun. It took only eight days for the advancing Axis forces to retake Benghazi and propel Ritchie's Eighth Army toward Tobruk in yet another phase of the "Benghazi Handicap," as easterly retreats had become facetiously referred to. Rommel had reversed his losses during Operation Crusader, and the British XIII Corps withdrew into the Gazala–Bir Hacheim defense line just west of Tobruk, albeit only partially repaired. Both sides regrouped extensively from early February until mid-May for a future offensive, but it was Rommel who took the initiative and attacked on May 26, which would start the Battle of Gazala.

Rommel outmaneuvered and outfought the Eighth Army, and after losing thousands of men, Ritchie's forces were compelled to retreat again. Tobruk was finally taken by the Axis along with vast quantities of supplies, equipment, and fuel. The German leader was given a field marshal's baton, and he was intent on driving straight across the Western Desert to Cairo and, perhaps, beyond. Auchinleck took over personal command of the Eighth Army from Ritchie and took up positions inside Egypt at Mersa Matruh on June 23, 1942. The ramifications of an Allied defeat were devastating. Should Rommel reach the Nile Delta and capture the Suez Canal, Hitler could toy with the idea of sending forces south from the Caucasus to link up with the now *Panzer-Armee Afrika* and then assault the oil fields of Iraq and Persia. After fighting for only two days at Mersa Matruh, Auchinleck, who had the intent to keep the Eighth Army intact to fight again, withdrew into a hastily prepared defensive line at El Alamein.

After this seesaw struggle since December 1940 between the British and Axis forces finally came to a stalemate after the First Battle of El Alamein in July 1942, where the multinational British Eighth Army—a conglomerate of British and Dominion forces from Australia, New Zealand, South Africa, India, Sudan, and Palestine, as well as expatriate soldiers from Greece, Poland, and Czechoslovakia—fought valiantly, Auchinleck had, indeed, successfully defended the Nile Delta at locales such as Deir el Shein, Tel el Eisa, Ruweisat Ridge, Bab el Qattar, Miteirya Ridge, and Tel El Mukh Khad. These Allied actions, although yielding mixed results, had the cumulative effect of stopping Rommel's *Panzer-Armee Afrika* along the coastal strip north of the Quattara Depression. Nonetheless, some of the Eighth Army's senior officers, including Auchinleck, were sacked by Churchill in August 1942 and replaced with Gen. Sir Harold R.L.G. Alexander as C-in-C Middle East, while command of the Eighth Army was ceded to Lt. Gen. Bernard Law Montgomery after Churchill's original command selection, Lt. Gen. William H.E. "Strafer" Gott, an old "desert hand" and commander of XIII Corps, met tragic circumstances. Gott, flying in from the desert to Cairo, had his plane attacked on landing at the airfield. While he was helping to remove wounded occupants from the plane, he was killed. Gott's XIII Corps command went to Lt. Gen. Brian Horrocks, while XXX and X Corps were led by Lt. Gen. Oliver Leese and Lt. Gen. Herbert Lumsden, respectively.

Alexander was held in the utmost esteem by the British prime minister, Winston Churchill, as the former presided over the last stages of the Dunkirk evacuation in June 1940 as well as the ignoble Burma retreat in the spring of 1942. During both catastrophes for British arms, Alexander had exhibited the requisite sangfroid of a commander as well as disengaging his defeated forces at the correct time from highly mobile enemy units. Alexander was ordered by Churchill to not preside over another British retreat but, rather, was instructed: "your prime and main duty will be to take or destroy at the earliest opportunity the German-Italian Army commanded by Field Marshal Rommel together with all its supplies and establishments in Egypt and Libya." Alexander's "weapon" was going to be Montgomery's reindoctrinated and revitalized Eighth Army. Montgomery's last battle command had been that of a division at Dunkirk, where he won the praise of the now CIGS, Gen. Sir Alan Brooke. Montgomery was fortunate in that his first encounter with Rommel's DAK and his Italian allies ended in a British victory at Alam Halfa in August 1942, although some have argued that it was based on defensive strategy that Auchinleck and his staff had originated earlier. The stage was now set in the Western Desert for the last conflict that would either break the Axis alliance knocking on the doorsteps of Alexandria and Cairo or cause a horrific defeat for the British that would probably cost them the Suez Canal and, perhaps, the oil fields of Iraq.

The Second Battle of El Alamein would finally end the nearly two-year battle for Egypt. On October 23, 1942, Montgomery ordered the largest artillery barrage, some 1,000 British guns, yet seen in the war to launch his Operation Lightfoot. Leese's XXX Corps attacked the northern minefields of Rommel's positions to also open a corridor for Lumsden's armor-rich X Corps. Facing Montgomery's 195,000 troops were 104,000 Axis troops, more than half of them Italians who were not as well armed as the Germans. The Eighth Army fielded more than 1,000 mostly superior tanks against fewer than 240 for the Germans and 280 obsolete models for the Italians. After almost three days of fighting, the German main defenses were yet to be penetrated. Lumsden was criticized by Montgomery for not wanting to risk his tanks being too far forward of the infantry. On October 26 the Australian 9th Division and the British 1st Armoured Division began to make some headway in the northern sector of the battle area. An enemy counterattack on the following day was repelled by the British 1st Armoured Division's and Australians' excellent use of their 6-pounder AT guns. On October 28–30 the 9th Australian Division continued to hammer at the northern salient, aiming for the coast. As Rommel responded by shifting his armor to the north to counter the Australians, Montgomery launched Operation Supercharge on November 1 to the south of the Australians. The next day a combined attack by New Zealand infantry and the 9th Armoured Brigade broke through the German defenses, enabling X Corps' armor to fight their way forward. From November 2–4 a battle of attrition inevitably "crumbled" the Axis defenses and *Panzer-Armee Afrika* forces begin their long retreat along the coastal road or to prisoner-of-war (POW) stockades.

After Second Alamein, even Rommel believed that the continued Axis presence in North Africa was a futile gesture, and he sought to convince Hitler to withdraw the *Panzer-Armee Afrika* while there was still a chance. He bluntly informed Hitler that "if the Army remained in North Africa it would be destroyed." Hitler rejected his field marshal's advice, and when Operation Torch commenced in Northwest Africa on November 8, 1942, the German Nazi leader appointed Gen. Hans-Jürgen von Arnim to lead a new panzer army in Tunisia after having received 100,000 German reinforcements to maintain a firm grip on French North Africa and a bridgehead in Tunis and Bizerte.

Even before Pearl Harbor, Roosevelt and Churchill considered Germany as a more dangerous threat to their countries and survival, and they had adopted a strategy to defeat Germany first. Although Allied planners entertained a number of possible sites for involvement in Europe by American forces after Pearl Harbor and Hitler's declaration of war on the United States, they were confronted with two competing plans as Hitler was moving on Egypt in North Africa and advancing uninterruptedly in the southern Soviet Union toward Stalingrad. The first, Operation Roundup, argued for an invasion of France in early 1943 and was favored by the American chairman of the Joint Chiefs of Staff, Gen. George C. Marshall, and his protégé in the War Plans Division, Brig. Gen. Dwight D. Eisenhower. Marshall wanted no part in a Mediterranean campaign and recognized that Northwest Europe would be the decisive battlefield. Churchill and Brooke dreaded a continental invasion against the mighty *Wehrmacht* so soon after their previous string of expeditionary disasters at Dunkirk and Narvik in 1940, in Greece in 1941, and at Dieppe in August 1942. The disastrous Dieppe amphibious assault taught the Allies that attacking a defended port was suicidal. Another failed invasion on a foreign shore might lead to the downfall of Churchill's government and impede Britain's continuation of the war. Thus, Churchill and the British planners favored Operation Torch, the invasion of French North Africa, which was weakly defended by Vichy French forces and colonial troops. Ultimately Marshall and Eisenhower were overruled and Roosevelt sided with the British on

Operation Torch being the main campaign for 1942 in the European Theater. Roosevelt was of the opinion that American combat forces should be committed as quickly as possible in the European Theater and would not accept a plan of action that was delayed until 1943.

By 1942 Eisenhower had so impressed Marshall that the latter promoted him to major general and sent him to England in the spring of 1942 to coordinate American planning with the British. Before the war the largest formation that Eisenhower had commanded was an infantry battalion as a lieutenant colonel in 1940. His meteoric rise was also aided by an appearance of affability, which underscored his commitment to fostering a cohesive Anglo-American alliance. It was Churchill who posed Eisenhower's name for the command of Operation Torch.

The scope of Torch was, indeed, geographically vast and operationally widespread. There were nine objectives along the thousand-mile coastal line of Northwest Africa that were to be amphibiously seized, with the three ports of Casablanca, Oran, and Algiers in French Morocco and Algeria being the chief targets. After the capture of the three principal ports, a lengthy overland assault was to be conducted to capture Bizerte and Tunis before von Arnim's *Wehrmacht* reinforcements arrived to strengthen the Nazi bridgehead in Tunisia. Simultaneous with this operation, Montgomery would continue his westward movement in an attempt to overtake and destroy Rommel's combined Italian and German forces before they could reach Tunisia and join with von Arnim's units.

American soldiers in a recently captured Japanese dugout in the vicinity of Buna on the northern coast of Papua New Guinea during the latter months of 1942. These infantrymen were with the U.S. 32nd ("Red Arrow") Infantry Division, a National Guard unit comprising mostly men from Michigan and Wisconsin. A veteran of this Buna campaign from Grand Rapids, Michigan, stated, "If I owned New Guinea and I owned hell, I would live in hell and rent out New Guinea." The Japanese defense of Papua in late 1942 to early 1943 was both suicidal and tenacious; however, MacArthur's decimated American and Australian infantry battalions defeated the enemy in that hellacious terrain, thereby eliminating the threat of another Japanese advance on Port Moresby from northern Papua. USAMHI

Temporally coincident with the Japanese southerly advance across the Owen Stanley Range and down the Kokoda Trail toward Port Moresby, the U.S. Marine Corps' 1st Division (Reinforced), under the command of Maj. Gen. Alexander A. Vandegrift, storm Beach Red unopposed on the northern coast of Guadalcanal on August 7, 1942, to capture the nearly completed enemy airfield on Lunga Plain.
USMC

Allied dignitaries and leaders gather aboard the HMS *Prince of Wales* in Placentia Bay, Newfoundland, as part of the Atlantic Conference on August 14, 1941. At that meeting the Atlantic Charter was issued as a joint Anglo-American declaration, although it would be several more months until the United States would enter the war as a combatant. These same leaders would grapple with where the Allies should conduct their first offensive in the European Theater almost a year later. Front row seated are U.S. president Franklin D. Roosevelt (left) and British prime minister Winston S. Churchill (right). Behind them standing (left to right) are Adm. Ernest J. King, commander in chief, U.S. Navy; Gen. George C. Marshall, U.S. Army chief of staff; and Field Marshal Sir John Dill, Britain's military representative to Washington. NARA

Two soldiers of the British Expeditionary Force use their rifles to shoot at low-flying German planes strafing the beaches as they wait to depart by small boat to larger ships off the coast of Dunkirk in late May–early June 1940. The forced evacuation occurred after the *Wehrmacht*'s devastating blitzkrieg through the Low Countries and northern France, which began on May 10, 1940. Both the British and French were completely unprepared for this newer type of mechanized continental warfare. AUTHOR'S COLLECTION

British troops man a Bren gun on a tripod as others remain on alert for a German aerial attack outside the Norwegian port of Narvik. On April 9, 1940, the Nazis invaded Denmark, forcing its capitulation within hours. Also on that date the Germans seized Oslo, Stavanger, Bergen, Trondheim, and Narvik in Norway. The British and French Allies decided to counterattack at Narvik on the urging of Winston Churchill, then First Lord of the Admiralty, although it lay within the Arctic Circle. The objective was to retake Narvik as a staging area to seize the Gallivåre iron ore fields in Sweden even though other Allied operations against the Germans in central Norway were proceeding badly. Despite a British naval victory over a German destroyer force in the Ofot Fiord leading into Narvik, the Allies had to eventually withdraw. AUTHOR'S COLLECTION

The beach at Dieppe along the French coast is strewn with dead Canadian infantrymen and disabled British Churchill tanks and landing craft after the failure of Operation Jubilee, which had as its objective the seizure of a Nazi-defended continental port by amphibious assault in August 1942. The prime minister's grandiloquent writings referred to it as "a costly but not unfruitful reconnaissance-in-force … tactically it was a mine of experience … revealing many shortcomings in our outlook … we learnt the value of heavy naval guns in an opposed landing." More than 1,000 men from the Canadian 2nd Division died on the beaches of Dieppe, with another 2,000 becoming POWs. Additionally, 106 of 650 RAF aircraft were destroyed, along with 33 of 179 landing craft lost at sea or on the beaches and 1 of 8 destroyers sunk, in addition to the deaths of 500 Royal Navy personnel. NARA

Benito Mussolini, the Italian Fascist dictator, who thrust his country into war as an Axis partner, first by invading France prior to the latter's surrender in June 1940 and then by sending the Italian Tenth Army across the Libyan frontier into Egypt against the British in September 1940. NARA

British commanders meet in Tobruk after the successful capture of that Cyrenaican port by Australian Imperial Force (AIF) 6th Division infantry in January 1941. On the left is Lt. Gen. Richard O'Connor, who developed the British counterattack, Operation Compass, and led it in December 1940 at the head of the Western Desert Force (renamed British XIII Corps on January 1, 1941). In the center is Gen. Archibald P. Wavell, C-in-C Middle East, who shared O'Connor's enthusiasm for the bold counterstroke. On the right is Maj. Gen. Iven G. Mackay, commander of the Australian 6th Division, which comprised O'Connor's infantry, after the successful 4th Indian Division was sent to Eritrea to combat the Italians there. AWM

Infantrymen of the AIF 6th Division race through the Libyan port of Bardia, which had an 18-mile perimeter and an Italian garrison of 45,000 men. The Australians assaulted this heavily defended port from late December 1940 to early January 1941. After the main defenses were penetrated by the Australians on January 3–5, 1941, Italian resistance crumbled to the onrushing Aussie infantry. More than 35,000 Italians were taken prisoner, along with numerous artillery pieces of all calibers. AWM

Italian prisoners march en masse to stockades after the wholesale surrender of Bardia as well as other locales such as Sidi Barrani. Mussolini's Tenth Army was destroyed, with those who escaped west heading for Tobruk during the first week of January 1941. NARA

AIF 6th Division AT units arrive in Tobruk after fighting through strongpoints along the 30-mile perimeter from January 8–21, 1941. The 2-pounder AT guns are mounted on Chevrolet 30-cwt trucks referred to as "portees." Tobruk had an Italian garrison of 25,000 men along with more than 200 guns and 65 light and medium tanks. AWM

A British Matilda Mk II Infantry (or I) tank from the 7th Battalion, Royal Tank Regiment (7th RTR), under Lt. Col. R.M. Jerram, with its .303-inch Besa machine guns and 2-pounders on the way to Derna after the conquest of Tobruk. These slow but heavily armored tanks were designed for infantrymen to be able to keep up with them rather than for rapid, mobile deployments. The tank's curious name was derived from a popular feathered cartoon character of the time, Matilda the Duck, because the tank's 27 tons of metal moved about as elegantly as an overweight waddling duck. These tanks devastated the Italian breastworks, or sangars, since they were able to take inordinate Italian AT gunfire. The famous British military columnist and author Capt. Sir Basil Liddell-Hart commented about the 7th RTR and its Matilda tanks, "the history of war shows no case of a single fighting unit having such a great effect in deciding the issue of battles." However, the Matilda only fired solid-shot armor-piercing shells, which was of little use against superior German AT guns, especially the vaunted German 88mm AA/AT artillery piece. Even the German 50mm PaK 38 AT gun could penetrate the front of a Matilda using composite rigid shot. When the Germans started using the 88mm AA guns against tanks, either in France or the Western Desert, it was clear that the Matilda had met its match. AWM

Australian infantry of the AIF 6th Division's 19th Brigade march through the civic square of Benghazi on February 7, 1941. The next day the main Australian column also marched in. As the Cyrenaican port city had many residents of Greek and Jewish ethnicity, the crowds greeted the "diggers" with an enthusiasm reserved for liberators. AWM

The Nazi leader, Adolf Hitler (left), meets with the Italian Fascist dictator, Benito Mussolini, at a railway station to review the dire situation in North Africa in regard to the British capture of Cyrenaica during Operation Compass and advances beyond. The German dictator assured Mussolini that he would send military assistance to reverse the war's events and to protect the southern flank of the Axis partnership. Hitler had already come to save a previous Italian military misadventure in Greece in late 1940, which resulted in the Axis conquest of that country in April 1941 after defeating local Greek military units and a hastily devised British expeditionary force. NARA

Gen. Erwin Rommel, in charge of a new *Wehrmacht* formation, the *Deutsches Afrikakorps* (DAK), arrives in Tripoli with the initial contingent of it, the 5th Light Motorized Division, which he reviews while standing in his Adler staff car in Tripoli on February 12, 1941. The term "DAK" would become official one week later. Rommel had a formidable reputation as an armored warfare commander, notably as a panzer division leader in northern France during the blitzkrieg of May 1940. Now the desert would provide the ideal terrain for him to exhibit his theories of combined arms in mechanized warfare, where the aim was destruction of enemy forces rather than seizure of locales. NARA

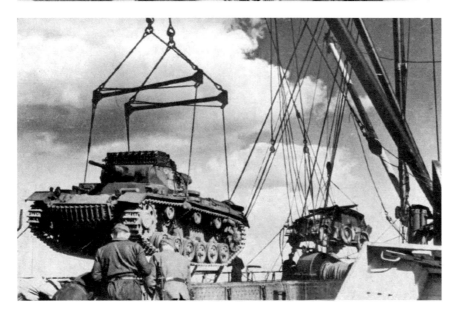

The arrival of General Rommel's Panzerkampfwagen (PzKpfw) III Ausf. G medium tanks being off-loaded from Axis transports in the harbor at Tripoli in February 1941. The German Panzer III battle tank mounted a 50mm L/42 gun with a performance comparable to that of the Matilda's 2-pounder. The Panzer III was the mainstay of Hitler's early offensives and in use with the DAK was far superior to any Allied armor before 1942. The DAK also had a smaller number of heavier Panzer IVs, which arrived at Tripoli in the early spring and carried a 75mm gun. German tanks carried a dual-purpose gun capable of firing armor-piercing and high-explosive rounds. AUTHOR'S COLLECTION

An Australian infantry company of the 2/13th Battalion, which had been the rearguard into Tobruk, mans defensive positions out on the perimeter on April 30, 1941. Rommel had surrounded the port of Tobruk on April 11 and placed it under siege; however, after hasty attacks over the ensuing week, his Axis forces were beaten off with considerable losses. On April 30 Rommel launched a major assault on Tobruk assisted by seventy tanks, but again it failed, with a loss of over a thousand Axis troops. AWM

An Australian Bren gun team, using a tripod for defense against low-flying Axis fighters, amid the rubble of one of Tobruk's buildings during the eight-month siege that ended on December 10, 1941. Larger guns were both ineffective and extremely vulnerable to low-flying aircraft. AWM

An Australian 2-pounder AT gun and crew in action at Tobruk in September 1941. Although this weapon was becoming obsolete, it was still effective against the more lightly-armored Italian tanks and could disable a German panzer at close range with a shot through a vulnerable tank position. However, out in the open, as such, these AT guns were easy targets for German tanks firing high-explosive shells. AWM

About to leave the relative safety of their perimeter position behind the barbed wire for a patrol in September 1941 are two Australian infantrymen of the 2/13th Battalion. The one on the left is carrying his Short Magazine Lee-Enfield (SMLE) .303-inch rifle with attached sword bayonet, while the one on the right holds his Thompson .45-cal submachine gun, which was initially devised for its "trench-clearing" capability but proved to have incredible stopping power against attacking infantry, albeit at shorter ranges. AWM

Tankers of the 6th Australian Cavalry Regiment crew Italian M13/40 (left) and M11/30 medium tanks (middle and foreground) that were seized after the capture of Bardia and then redesignated with the kangaroo emblem. These tanks were transported to Tobruk for use in that port's seizure in January 1941 and subsequent defense beginning in April 1941. AWM

An Australian artillery crew uses a captured Italian AA gun against the almost incessant Axis air attacks on Tobruk during the siege. More than 200 Italian artillery pieces were captured by the Australians when they captured Tobruk in January 1941, along with many M11 and M14 tanks, which they also incorporated into their defense during the siege. When faced with massed aerial assault, AA gunners had their guns facing outward covering a 360° arc of defense, which along with the use of short fuse lengths would force enemy aircraft to move to a higher altitude to minimize losses. About 300 Axis planes were either shot down, damaged, or listed as probable hits; however, captured German documents revealed that this figure was an underestimate of actual Axis aircraft losses. AWM

Two German Ju 87 *Sturzkampfflugzeugs* (dive-bombers, abbreviated as *Stukas*) descend to attack shipping in the port of Tobruk despite a curtain of ack-ack provided by the Australian gunners below. Such limited sorties as well as massed *Stuka* attacks became commonplace, albeit frightful, among Tobruk's defenders within the perimeter. AWM

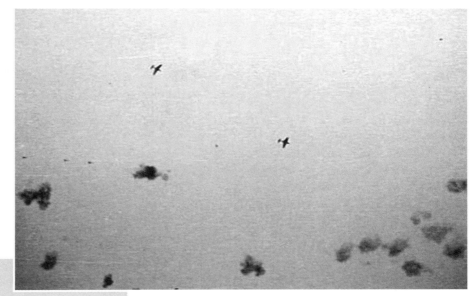

A Ju 87 *Stuka* stands idle in the desert after it was forced to land because of Australian AA gunfire. The *Stukas* suffered heavily in the skies over Tobruk. The *Stuka* exhibited gull-like wings and nonretractable, massive landing gear as shown. The plane first flew in service in 1935 and saw action in the Spanish Civil War. It could carry over 1,000 kilograms of bombs and was modified for service in North Africa with sand filters. In addition to its precision bombing, with an aircrew of two, this aircraft possessed screaming dive trumpets, which instilled terror in any recipient of a *Stuka* dive-bombing attack. However, the plane was slow and as a dive-bomber was extremely vulnerable coming out of its descent. AWM

A Panzer PzKpfw II light tank that was destroyed by an Australian soldier hurling a "Molotov cocktail" incendiary at it and setting it ablaze within the Tobruk perimeter in April 1941. This tank was vastly inferior in both its 35mm maximum armored protection and its 20mm KwK 30 or 38 turret gun (depending on the model), along with a 7.92mm machine gun as its armament. AWM

A Mark VI A15 Cruiser tank, the "Crusader." It weighed 19 tons and had a crew of five. Although it was much speedier than the Matilda I tank, it had similar armaments, with two 7.92mm Besa machine guns and only the 2-pounder turret gun, which, likewise, fired only shot and not high-explosive rounds. Thus, it was grossly inadequate against German armor, and with only 40mm of frontal armor, it was an easy target of German AT guns, especially the "88." The desert terrain did not help with its overall mechanical unreliability. AWM

Gen. Sir Claude Auchinleck (in middle without a service hat) stands among AIF senior officers in Syria in October 1941. Auchinleck, who performed well in northern Norway during the Narvik evacuation in 1940, had replaced General Wavell as C-in-C Middle East after the unsuccessful Operations Battleaxe and Brevity, both of which failed to drive Rommel's DAK away from the Egyptian frontier in June 1941. Prior to becoming C-in-C Middle East, Auchinleck was C-in-C India, after having an excellent career as a regular officer in the Indian Army. In addition, he won the respect of Prime Minister Winston Churchill for his prompt action in sending the 10th Indian Division to Basra in southern Iraq, in order to protect the oil fields there and advance up the Euphrates River to Baghdad between April and June 1941 after the Nazi-inspired Iraq Rebellion had erupted on April 1, 1941. AWM

A column of Allied soldiers, many of them South Africans under the command of Maj. Gen. Hendrik Klopper, march into captivity under the watchful eye of a DAK soldier after the port city and perimeter of Tobruk fell to the Germans with the surrender of the garrison on June 21, 1942. The loss of Tobruk was disastrous, with more than 33,000 South African, Indian, and British troops captured. More than 2,000 Allied vehicles were also seized and put into Axis service. AUTHOR'S COLLECTION

Gen. Claude Auchinleck (left), C-in-C Middle East and in nominal charge of Eighth Army since the debacle at Gazala, stands on the Via Balbia with an officer from the British 50th Division during the retreat from Gazala to Alamein. Auchinleck failed to receive just credit for his series of attacks and defensive stands against the DAK near Alamein during July 1942 (the First Battle of El Alamein), which threw Rommel's offensive off course, necessitating the German commander to suspend his drive for the Suez Canal, Alexandria, and Cairo and construct his own defensive line. AUTHOR'S COLLECTION

A sign marks the railway station at Alamein, where some Australian "digger" irreverently, but comically, engraved the word "Heaven" on the masonry wall. On June 26, 1942, Auchinleck canceled his order for a stand at the Eighth Army desert base of Mersa Matruh after a two-day running battle with the DAK and instructed his formations to retire to the El Alamein line, which had some partial defensive preparations made. AWM

A 25-pounder field artillery piece of the Australian 2/8th Field Regiment of the Royal Australian Artillery fires at DAK positions along the coastal sector during the First Battle of El Alamein in mid-July 1942. AWM

Australian 9th Division artillery spotters, in a forward observation trench at Tel El Eisa, Egypt, assess the effects of rounds landing near enemy positions in July 1942. AWM

Australian 9th Infantry Division troops use a captured Italian Breda 47/32 M25 AT gun just after Rommel's attack on Montgomery's position at Alam Halfa, in an attempt by the DAK commander to get past a resurgent Eighth Army into Egypt. AWM

A Vickers Mk I machine gun position, manned by 9th Australian Division infantrymen, fires in an indirect supportive role at Tel El Eisa, Egypt, in July 1942. This particular crew fired their venerable, water-cooled weapon, which had a cyclic rate of fire of 600 rounds per minute utilizing .303-inch caliber ammunition, almost continuously for two days, and as a result their hands were burned from the heated barrel after their water supply was gone. Although this machine gun entered service with the British Army in 1912, later modifications gave this machine gun a range of almost 2 miles. AWM

A private from the 9th Australian Infantry Division waits in his dugout position with his 3-inch mortar at his side at Tel El Eisa, Egypt, on August 1, 1942. From July 26–27 the Australians began an attack from Tel El Eisa toward DAK positions on the Miteirya Ridge; however, after almost a month of frequent engagements, both were well established in defensive positions and near exhaustion. The attack failed to dent the DAK line, and Auchinleck suspended the offensive to strengthen his line and rest his troops. AWM

British prime minister Winston Churchill stands at the left in his tropical sun helmet and with his trademark cigar in his mouth at an Eighth Army base in the Egyptian desert in mid-August 1942. With him are Maj. Gen. Leslie Morshead (middle), commander of the AIF 9th Infantry Division, and Gen. Sir Claude Auchinleck (right), C-in-C Middle East, who had been in nominal command of the Eighth Army since the defeat at Gazala, where General Ritchie was relieved of command. Churchill was not in good spirits with the previous loss of Tobruk and now a stalemate in Egypt, and like his predecessor Wavell, Auchinleck lacked a good communication channel with the prime minister. To that end Gen. Sir Harold Alexander was ordered to replace Auchinleck as C-in-C Middle East while Lt. Gen. Bernard L. Montgomery took over the Eighth Army. AWM

Lt. Gen. Bernard L. Montgomery after assuming command of the Eighth Army in mid-August 1942 wearing an Australian slouch hat that was given to him. Montgomery added the various badges of his Eighth Army units to the hat. Prior to being given the desert command, Montgomery was in charge of Southeastern Army in England. Lt. Gen. William "Strafer" Gott, who had been in the Western Desert since the outbreak of the war and was in command of XIII Corps at Gazala, was supposed to get the Eighth Army command; however, he died when his plane was forced to land and was subsequently machine-gunned by the Germans. Thus, through serendipity, Montgomery instead would take over Eighth Army and replace some of its commanders with men that he knew to reenergize the Commonwealth troops for the upcoming defensive battle at Alam Halfa (August 31–September 4) and the offensive at Second Alamein, which was to commence on October 23. AWM

On October 23, 1942, Montgomery fired the largest artillery barrage seen during WWII up until that time to herald the commencement of Operation Lightfoot. Here a 4.5-inch Royal Artillery field gun fires during the night as part of the bombardment. On average the 4.5-inch guns fired 102 rounds per gun per day over the initial twelve days of fighting during Second Alamein. More than 1 million rounds were fired by the British field guns, which included the 25-pounders and 5.5-inch weapons as well. AWM

Infantrymen, with fixed sword bayonets, of the AIF 9th Division advance through a smokescreen onto an Axis strongpoint that was holding up their progress on November 3, 1942. Montgomery used his Australian contingents, beginning on the night of October 24, to begin "crumbling" Axis defenses on the northern or right flank of the offensive toward the sea with the intent of seizing the coastal road by surprising the enemy. Morshead's infantry succeeded in capturing many strategic battlefield targets. AWM

A U.S.-manufactured M4A1 medium, or Sherman, tank in British service races through the desert at Second Alamein. The initial contingent of Sherman tanks arrived just in time to participate in Montgomery's pivotal October/November offensive. The M4A1 also equaled any German tank in subsequent engagements in Tunisia until confrontations with the German Mk VI "Tiger" demonstrated the latter's clear superiority. NARA

A British 6-pounder AT gun in action with an enemy high-explosive round landing precariously nearby. This excellent AT gun arrived in North Africa in mid-1942 in time for the Gazala battle and proved vital at both Alamein battles and Alam Halfa against German and Italian tanks. The 6-pounder shell could penetrate 50mm of armor at approximately 1,650 yards. American factories made a 57mm AT gun, which had the same design as the British 6-pounder. The arrival of the British 6-pounder also enabled the 25-pounder field artillery piece to revert to its primary function rather than function in an AT role due to the obsolete performance of the 2-pounder AT gun. AUTHOR'S COLLECTION

Two DAK infantrymen in a slit trench on the Alamein front. One is holding binoculars while the other fires his rifle at low-flying Allied aircraft. With limited panzer reserves and fuel for them, DAK senior officers had to rely heavily on the élan of the German infantrymen to combat Montgomery's numerical superiority in both men and matériel. AWM

Two DAK Panzer (PzKpfw) Mk III tanks lie disabled near Tel El Eisa, Egypt. The Mk III is easily identified in its profile by its six bogey wheels. This panzer model was the mainstay of the DAK and its earlier offensives in 1941–42 and consistently outperformed British armor until the arrival of the M3 and M4 medium tanks with their 75mm guns in the sponson and traversable turret positions, respectively. AWM

A captured Russian 76.2mm M1936 field gun sits atop a *Sd.Kfz.* 251/7 semitracked or half-track vehicle to perform as a self-propelled artillery vehicle in the DAK 605th AT Battalion. The captured 76.2mm Russian artillery piece was also mounted on a Panzer II chassis to create a *Panzerjäger* 38(t) and was used in the spring of 1942 as a self-propelled AT gun. AWM

A crashed German Messerschmitt Bf 109F fighter lies on the desert floor with a British Hurricane fighter circling above. German planes of this type inflicted heavy losses on inferior Allied aircraft, such as the Curtiss P-40 Kittyhawks. However, with the arrival of Hurricane and then Spitfire RAF squadrons, the competitive edge of the Bf 109 was eroded. The Bf 109F entered service in the spring of 1941 and exhibited the best attributes of the Bf 109 series of models. The Bf 109F had two 7.92mm machine guns and a fixed, forward-firing 15 or 20mm cannon depending on the prototype in the F series. AWM

Infantrymen of the AIF 9th Division race with bayonets fixed toward Germans surrendering in a strongpoint in the northern sector of Montgomery's Alamein offensive front. Morshead's infantry were assigned the task of driving through to the coast, as is evident by the Mediterranean in the background. AWM

Italian POWs captured by Australians on the first day of Montgomery's Alamein offensive march to the rear in formation to commence captivity in stockades prior to more permanent prisoner camps remote from Africa. AWM

In late January 1942 Brig. Gen. Dwight D. Eisenhower (left), the new chief of war plans for the Army's General Staff, and the Army chief of staff, General George C. Marshall (right), who appointed him to the post, discuss a blueprint for Army operations in the European Theater of Operations. Eisenhower wrote at that time, "We've got to go to Europe and fight … We've got to quit wasting resources all over the world … and still worse … wasting time." Marshall could not have agreed more with his protégé's concepts, as both argued for an early infusion of American soldiers to staging areas in Britain in 1942 (Operation Bolero) as part of a plan for a cross-channel invasion of France in April 1943 (Operation Roundup). The British partner in the alliance demurred at another European invasion after Dunkirk, Narvik, and Greece, as well as what was to become another disaster, Dieppe in August 1942. The British CIGS, Gen. Sir Alan Brooke, harbored grave reservations that if British troops invaded Continental Europe prematurely they would be hastily expelled, yet again, with unacceptably high casualties. NARA

American president Franklin D. Roosevelt (left) and British prime minister Winston S. Churchill (right) in an iconic image of the Allies discussing strategy in Casablanca after the successful Operation Torch landings and continuation of the Tunisian offensive. Churchill was instrumental in swaying Roosevelt's enthusiasm away from a French invasion in 1943 and getting his consent, against his military planners' advice, for the invasion of Northwest Africa instead. Roosevelt, the consummate politician, wanted to help the Russians as soon as possible with all the clamoring for a "Second Front" stateside, especially as fighting in and around Stalingrad on the Volga River was to reach a crescendo. To accomplish this, he had to expeditiously involve American soldiers in some offensive action in the European Theater in 1942, as he did at Guadalcanal with the 1st Marine Division and U.S. Navy in August 1942 and in Papua New Guinea with General MacArthur in November 1942. He also thought that an invasion of Northwest Africa would move Vichy France closer to the Anglo-American alliance. NARA

CHAPTER 2
GEOGRAPHY, TERRAIN, AND THE INVASION

The nature of a military theater's terrain lies at the heart of the tactics and weaponry employed and further developed experientially. Terrain features enable an experienced soldier to increase the power of a defensive position or, conversely, to select the most suitable path for an offensive. For any campaign or operation, geography stands in sharp contrast to terrain. Germane to military parlance, geography examines the relationship of one locale to another, in regard to distance, size, and value of the point of focus, as well as how suitable lines of communication will be. Thus, military geography serves to dictate strategic decision making and necessitates particular logistics to achieve those plans. Both terrain and geography became pivotal aspects of the planning, the landings, and, ultimately, the race for Tunis, which the Allies viewed as the prize of Operation Torch.

The Northwest African countries within French North Africa, comprising French Morocco, Algeria, and Tunisia, had remained virtually untouched by land combat between December 1940 and November 1942, while ceaseless fighting raged between Britain and her dominions versus the Axis partners across the Libyan and Egyptian deserts to the east during this interval. The nomadic Berbers continued their itinerant activity, while French colonial farmers grew their crops along the coastal plain. German or Italian troops were not present, and the French garrisons, mostly colonial, in the principal communities were certainly not on a war footing. The French, tending to their colonies, had developed ports, railroads, waterworks, power plants, and highways. There were several French naval bases and airfields. Many of Northwest Africa's key cities—Casablanca, Oran, Algiers, Bizerte, and Tunis—looked like their counterparts in metropolitan France.

The geographic scope of Operation Torch on November 8, 1942, was daunting, to say the least. The Allies had brought more than 110,000 men, 75 percent of them American, across the oceans and seas to the shores of Northwest Africa in two huge armadas—comprising more than 500 American and British warships, supply vessels, and troop transports—and in three simultaneous landings placed them ashore, from west to east, on beaches in proximity to Casablanca, Oran, and Algiers. The Casablanca-bound convoy (Western Task Force) sailed from the United States, while the Oran (Center Task Force) and Algiers (Eastern Task Force) amphibious armadas departed from ports in the United Kingdom. This invasion force had been assembled with great haste, utilizing mostly newly trained, non-battle-hardened troops, and sent across thousands of miles of ocean known to be infested with Axis submarines to storm disparate target destinations.

The Western Task Force was to depart from different ports on the East Coast of the United States, under the command of Rear Adm. H. Kent Hewitt, at different times beginning on October 3, 1942, to baffle Axis agents. The distance for this task force's journey to Morocco was 4,500 miles. The force was subdivided into three amphibious attack groups, in addition to a warship escort and a carrier air group, the latter consisting of the USS *Ranger* and three escort carriers screened by nine destroyers and a light cruiser. Most of the troop transports left Hampton Roads, Virginia, on October 23, while the warships ultimately sailed from Bermuda via Casco Bay in Maine. The Western Task Force made a rendezvous on October 28 and comprised a large convoy of nine long seaborne columns of transports led by a warship, which were to eventually land their assaulting soldiers at three invasion sites on either side of Casablanca.

As for the Center and Eastern Task Forces, most of the supply ships after loading assembled in the Firth of Clyde on October 17. After the transports arrived after a final rehearsal off the coast of Scotland, they joined the remaining ships for the passage through the Strait of Gibraltar. Two aircraft carriers escorted the Algiers-bound Eastern Task Force, while the Oran-bound Center Task Force had a battleship and an aircraft carrier as well as two escort carriers among numerous other smaller warships. In all, 340 vessels in the two task forces arrived at Gibraltar and passed uneventfully through the narrow strait in proper order. The journey from Scotland for these task forces was over 2,000 miles.

The distance from Casablanca to Tunis by road is just over 1,250 miles. Eisenhower's directive for Operation Torch amounted to assaulting and eventually seizing more than a million square miles of enemy-occupied territory. Because of the unfavorable geographical conditions, the population is concentrated in a small part of the total area, principally the ports. Apart from fairly flat and open coast on the Atlantic, most of the country running north-northeast toward the Mediterranean Sea consists of great chains of the high and rocky Atlas Mountains. South of this mountain range, the land falls away to desert punctuated with patches of local vegetation as the only ground cover and eventually the great Sahara.

The beaches of the Atlantic coast are beaten by high surf through which it is rarely possible to land a boat. The Mediterranean coastline is mainly rocky and cliff-lined. On the Mediterranean side from a point opposite Gibraltar to another about 150 miles to the east, a crescent-shaped mountain mass effectively bars access to the interior. Thence, eastward as far as Tunisia, coastal ranges, occasionally interrupted by plains, narrow river valleys, or wadis, drop sharply into the Mediterranean. The interior country is also marked by mountain range passes, such as at Kasserine, which can be dry or wet depending on the time of year. Thus, an essential for any landing operation along the Mediterranean coastline must be to capture ports, since maintenance and building up of the fighting forces that land amphibiously cannot be achieved over the beaches.

A military reason for setting a date before the winter of 1942 was the probability that by early November the winter weather on the Eastern Front, with the attendant reduction in a *Wehrmacht* offensive, would permit the *Luftwaffe* to transfer some of its planes back to Western Europe, and perhaps North Africa and Sicily. Also, the rainy season in Algeria and Tunisia starts early in November, with valleys becoming quagmires and ground becoming impossible for tracked vehicles and even infantry. One hydrographic issue centered on the west coast of French Morocco, as it was battered by high surf and heavy swell rolling in from the Atlantic. In October and November amphibious craft could safely beach on one day out of four. As it was, the surf at Fedala just to the north of Casablanca was only moderate, and the assault would go on as planned. With rough surf and strong winds, there was the potential for interference with carrier air operations, so acquisition of airfields in French Morocco and Algeria during the initial days of the invasion became paramount.

Casablanca surpassed all other ports in area, depth, loading facilities, and storage capacity. It handled almost 90 percent of Morocco's prewar traffic and served as the gateway for overseas shipments to all Northwest Africa. Lesser ports were Safi, Rabat-Sale, Mehdia, and Port-Lyautey, the last of which was an artificial port several miles up the shallow Sebou River from its mouth at Mehdia that had been dredged and constructed. The railroad system that linked these ports with the hinterland and with Algeria and Tunisia had as its main line a standard-gauge, partly electrified route that ran from Marrakech through Casablanca, Rabat-Sale, and Port-Lyautey to Oujda. One branch ran to Safi, a second to Tangier, and others to interior communities. Invading forces of any size would need to control the ports of Safi, Casablanca, and Port-Lyautey.

The Algerian coast has few points at which plains or valleys lead inland from the wide bays. At those sites, though, artificial ports have been constructed or natural harbors improved. The best unloading facilities and railroad connections were at Oran, Algiers, Bougie, Philippeville, and Bône, the latter being only 120 miles from Tunis and thus viewed as the desired location to achieve on D-Day. The main line of railroad ran eastward from Oujda, near the Moroccan boundary, through Tlemcen to Oran, thence through interior valleys some 20 miles south of the coast to Algiers, and then it crossed northern Tunisia to Bizerte and through Medjez el Bab to Tunis.

Logistical and infrastructural facts made it desirable to get amphibious assault troops on the ground as far east as possible in the Mediterranean, as the narrow-gauge railroads, with several short branches southward into central and southern Tunisia, would offer limited means to any large-scale movement for forces invading Tunisia overland from the west. Northwest Africa had poor communications, and a single standard-gauge railway ran for 600 miles from the Atlantic coast to Oran, another 250 miles to Algiers and a further 500 miles to Tunis. A narrow-gauge railway connected central Algeria with the Tunisian coast. To utilize the railways, the Allies would have to bring in extensive equipment and stores.

There were two east-west-running surface roads capable of taking two-way traffic with bridges with a twenty-five-ton capacity—one following the line of the Mediterranean coast and one parallel to it but farther inland. These would need to be employed to overcome deficient railroad supply. However, secondary roads lacked surfacing or drainage; thus they would be adequate only if favorable weather prevailed. The mountainous terrain inland prohibited cross-country routing of transport. These factors amplified the need to seize usable ports on the first assault.

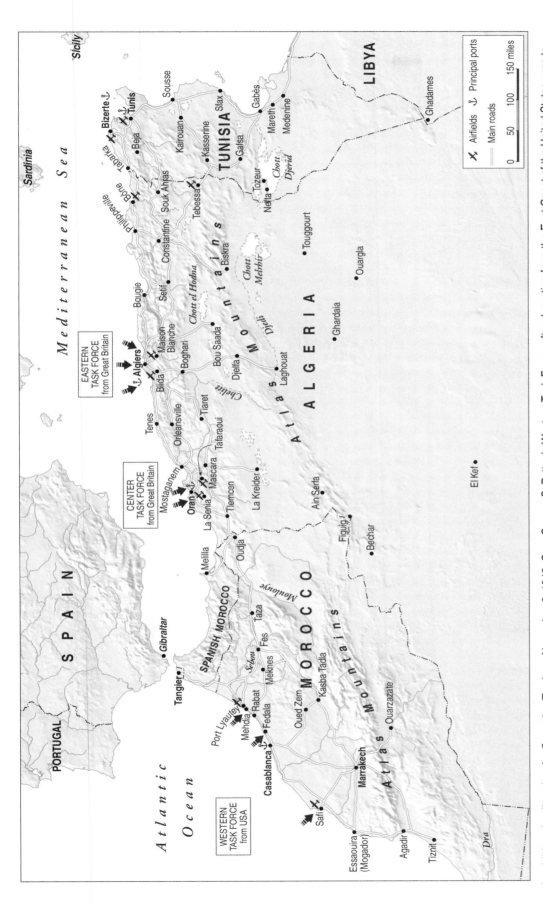

Amphibious landing sites for Operation Torch on November 8, 1942. Gen. George S. Patton's Western Task Force, after departing from the East Coast of the United States, was to make separate assaults at three different areas on Morocco's Atlantic coast, at Safi, Fedala, and Mehdia. The intent was to capture key airfields and converge on Casablanca, the main port objective, from inland. The Center and Eastern Task Forces, after passing uneventfully through the Strait of Gibraltar from embarkation points in Great Britain, would attack the main Algerian ports of Oran and Algiers, respectively, in a similar fashion by assaulting landing beaches astride the cities and then converging on them from inland routes. After the ports' capture and capitulation of the Vichy forces, followed by an immediate Allied buildup after D-Day, a newly designated British First Army of Anglo-American composition, under Lt. Gen. Kenneth Anderson, would undertake the invasion's next objective. The British First Army's task was to race 500 miles to the east and capture the port of Tunis, thereby preventing it from falling into German hands, as well as control the rest of Tunisia as Gen. Bernard Montgomery's Eighth Army advanced from the east. MERIDIAN MAPPING

The farther east that the Allies intended to land, as exemplified by Bône, the greater the risk of attack by Axis air units. Seizure of these ports would require a vigorous air presence for defense from Axis aerial assault if losses were to be kept within tolerable limits. However, large quantities of suitable Allied fighters to defend these more eastern ports were not readily available. Also at play was the belief that the Germans would move rapidly from Sicily to reinforce Tunis and possibly nearby ports, such as Bône. Finally, there were simply not enough troops to add Bône as an eastern port to seize.

From geographical and terrain perspectives, behind the coastal plain of Tunisia and across to its western frontier with Algeria, the Atlas Mountains have two spurs, the Western and Eastern Dorsal ranges, that run from the northern coast down to the salt marshes in the south. If an immediate Allied drive for Tunis failed, they would construct a line along the Eastern Dorsal by December 1942, and the only way for the Axis forces to pierce it would be to go around the southern portion of it at Gafsa or by trekking through the mountain passes at Pichon, Fondouk, Faïd, and Maknassy. The Western Dorsal is the smaller of the two ranges, joining the Eastern one in the north and then diverging to the southwest leading to Thelepte and Feriana. The Western Dorsal has

passes at Maktar, Sbiba, Kasserine, and Feriana. The two ranges on a map form a large inverted, V-shaped structure with the vertex pointing to the north. The passes could be blocked with relatively small forces, and for the Axis to get into the Allied rear echelon and lines of communication, they would have to first pass through the Eastern Dorsal and then through the Western Dorsal.

The topography of northeastern Tunisia is quite complex. Bizerte and Tunis are situated in coastal flatlands punctuated by hills that project to the coast from tall and irregularly shaped mountains, which are situated to the west. Bizerte's basin is relatively small, and much of it is submerged under the Lac de Bizerte and the marshy Garaet El Ichkeul. The plain adjacent to Tunis is separated from that of Bizerte and is bounded on the northwest, west, and south by the eastern extremities of high mountain ridges.

In sum, the rugged and barren nature of the terrain as well as some urban locales during the conflict in Northwest Africa would necessitate innovative solutions for infantry to maneuver amid harsh surroundings and climate as well as seek cover from artillery and air assault; for gunners to secure their weapons speedily and safely; and for armored vehicles to remain mobile, let alone obtain the best positioning for firing on the enemy.

Senegalese colonial troops serving under Vichy France present arms at a dress formation on a major street with streetcar tracks in Algiers on November 11, 1942, marking a cessation of hostilities between Adm. François Darlan's forces and the Anglo-American troops of the Eastern Task Force that amphibiously landed three days previously. Contrary to the public's perception stateside, Northwest Africa possessed several metropolitan port cities under Vichy French control. USAMHI

A trio of American soldiers stroll down a main Oran street in Algeria, just days after a mechanized task force crashed through toward the city's government buildings after the amphibious assault by the Center Task Force on November 8, 1942. Since this was the first combat for American soldiers in the European Theater and because it involved urban fighting, replacements and new units sent to Northwest Africa would receive training in house-to-house fighting. USAMHI

The metropolitan port of Algiers before the Eastern Task Force's amphibious landings. This city was the political and administrative seat of French North Africa under control of the Vichy government led by Marshal (Henri) Philippe Pétain since the armistice with the Nazis in June 1940. In Algiers at the time of the invasion was Admiral Darlan, who was the successor to Pétain in the pro-German regime, after he had held a number of titles including naval minister and prime minister. NARA

Tunis fell to the Allies at 3:30 P.M. on May 7, 1943. British vanguard troops of the Derbyshire Yeomanry and the 11th Hussars raced into the city and encountered some sporadic sniper fire that led to some firefights. Allied troops entering Tunis on May 8 staged an ad hoc parade of military vehicles—including trucks, Morris Quad tractors pulling field artillery pieces, and British Churchill tanks—to the gleeful cheers of the city's residents. Although the intact buildings along this narrow street route were representative of how much of the city was unscathed by war, the docks of Tunis were wrecked by Allied bombing. Tunis was the site of Hitler's initial reaction to the Torch landings, as he used the port city as a bridgehead on November 11, 1942, to bring in German and Italian reinforcements. In the eyes of the German dictator, this city would be viewed as "Tunisgrad". USAMHI

French colonial infantry march through an Algerian village street with their pack mules. On D-Day, November 8, 1942, villages such as these had to be seized by the amphibious forces on their way from the several landing beaches to invest the larger port cities of Casablanca, Oran, and Algiers since direct assaults were considered too hazardous. In fact, limited direct port attacks were made with small contingents to prevent sabotage of dock facilities for later use; however, these met with heavy defensive fire from French shore batteries and warships in port, leading to excessive casualties without success. NARA

German prisoners march along a Tunisian coastal road after their surrender in Tunisia during the second week of May. In the background are the orderly rows of olive trees planted by and tended to by the local French colonists. Sometimes these sites were used to conceal smaller artillery pieces for an ambush or to camouflage supply dumps from aerial attack by either side. NARA

A nomadic Bedouin atop his camel talks to a trio of American soldiers along a desolate area of flat Tunisian countryside. The GIs are wearing their long winter woolen trench coats during the cold Tunisian winter, especially at higher elevations of the mountain ranges. The Allies had envisioned a quick dash by the British First Army after the Eastern Task Force captured Algiers that would, likewise, yield Bizerte and Tunis by Christmas 1942. However, Axis reinforcements and counterattacks from Tunisia stalled the Allies, who had to call off their offensive until warmer weather, drier ground, reinforcements, and aerial support could be provided. NARA

A mechanized column of M3 medium Lee tanks of the 1st Armored Division moves through the desert plain toward fighting at Sened as some smoke billows in the background during the third week of March 1943. The attack had to be postponed due to the rainy weather, resulting in overflowing streams, flooded areas, and muddy roads, which hindered an armored advance. As seen by the tank tracks in the right foreground, the ground has dried out for the most part; however, a deep tread mark is still left in place. NARA

A mechanized column of M3 medium Lee tanks moves eastward along the valley floor for the Kasserine counteroffensive. The M3 Lee tanks were used after the M4 and M4A1 of the 2nd Battalion, 1st Armored Regiment of the 1st Armored Division suffered high losses during Gen. Hans-Jürgen von Arnim's 10th Panzer Division attack at Sidi Bou Zid on February 15, 1943. About twenty M4 Sherman tanks were destroyed that day by a battalion of Mk VI "Tiger" tanks of the 10th Panzer Division. Fortunately for these advancing M3 Lee tanks, there were limited numbers of Tiger tanks in use in Tunisia. NARA

Armored vehicles coursing through the North Africa desert terrain generated much dust as well as the occasional sandstorm or *khamaseen*. Here a tanker of the Royal Tank Regiment wears his protective goggles on his forehead out of the desert but still has the rest of his face begrimed by the fine sand dust. AWM

A reinforcing M3 medium Lee tank of the 2/13th Armored Regiment of the 1st Armored Division crosses Tunisian terrain occasionally dotted by a cactus plant during the third week of February 1943 to bolster other armored units after the combat near Sbeitla, where von Arnim's attacking panzers inflicted heavy casualties on 1st Armored Division defenses in the olive groves around that town. USAMHI

A pair of tank tracks demonstrates the path that an Allied tank took through the cactus plants; a mechanized column is present in the background, as well as billowing smoke indicating recent combat and vehicles ablaze. NARA

A dense clustering of cactus plants enables Italian gunners to conceal their 47/32 M37 antitank (AT) gun as it waits in ambush for an Allied mechanized column. This was the standard Italian infantry AT gun, which was obsolete by 1943. There was no gun shield, and the weapon could be quickly dismantled into a handful of component parts for transportation to a new site. As is evident, its low profile made it difficult to detect in the open and almost impossible in a concealed locale as above. AUTHOR'S COLLECTION

An American officer goes over a map with two tankers in a thicket of cactus plants, which thrive in the arid Tunisian soil. Instead of serving as a hedge or providing a foodstuff with their fruit, the plants offer some camouflage in the open, protecting the trio somewhat from aerial strafing by enemy fighters. NARA

British soldiers of the 7th Rifle Brigade crouch inconspicuously in a Tunisian wheat field in the Kounine Hills near Sousse, where there is arable land for this crop to grow. Here it serves to conceal advancing infantry before an attack in April 1943. The 7th Rifle Brigade was part of the British 1st Armored Division's 7th Motor Brigade in Montgomery's Eighth Army. NARA

The high peaks of the Atlas Mountains of North Africa stand majestically in the background. This mountain range stretches across Northwest Africa, extending almost 1,600 miles through Morocco, Algeria, and Tunisia, and serves to separate the Mediterranean and Atlantic coastlines from the Sahara Desert. The highest peak is Jebel Toubkal at 13,671 feet in southwestern Morocco. The Atlas Mountain range was the home of the Berbers, nomadic Arabs. NARA

An American B-25 Mitchell bomber of the Twelfth Air Force on a mission over the Atlas Mountains in Tunisia. In the background lies the valley floor, through which Allied and Axis mechanized forces would fight one another seeking either to defend or to crash through mountain passes to disrupt the vital supply lines of enemy forces. Mere possession of a pass by one side offered a threat to the other. NARA

A Tunisian hill (e.g., Hill 609), which served as a strategic defense position for Axis forces trying to prevent the Allies from reaching the ports of Bizerte and Tunis, demonstrates how it could be not only a strong enemy redoubt but also an excellent enemy observation position to direct artillery and air sorties. A belt of rugged enemy-controlled hill country, 15 to 20 miles in depth, lay between the American II Corps lines and Mateur, a center of enemy communications and key to the Bizerte area, in April and May 1943. The valleys offered little or no cover, with Axis artillery overlooking the Allied movements and dispositions. NARA

The 1st Ranger Battalion, commanded by Maj. William O. Darby, a thirty-one-year-old former artilleryman, hikes on a "speed march" across the undulating Algerian hills after their successful amphibious landing at Arzew to help seize two French forts that were covering Beach Z, 16 miles from Oran. Their next mission would be a raid on an Italian outpost at Sened Station in southern Tunisia. NARA

The 2nd Battalion of the U.S. 16th Infantry Division marches along a road through the Kasserine Pass after engineers had cleared it of mines following Rommel's withdrawal through it in late February 1943. Rommel ordered the retreat after his aborted attempt to get through British armored and artillery units into Thala to the northwest or break through elements of the 1st Armored Division and head west for Tebessa. NARA

The Kasserine Pass and its surrounding terrain, with roads leading to Thala and Tebessa on the left and right, respectively. The Hatab River was dry at the time of this photograph, with its evident riverbed in the foreground. AUTHOR'S COLLECTION

An M4A1 medium Sherman tank crosses a dry riverbed in the Sidi Bou Zid area, which was the site of von Arnim's enveloping attack on February 14, 1943, after breaking through the Faïd Pass. NARA

A British Valentine tank of the Eighth Army's 50th Royal Tank Regiment, in support of the 51st Highland Division, is immobilized in the muddy bottom of Wadi Zigzaou despite fascines laid out across it, delaying an attack on Axis positions near the Mareth Line. This terrain feature was difficult to traverse for both tanks and infantry and disrupted the timetable of Montgomery's advance. NARA

American jeeps travel on a rain-soaked Tunisian road. The wet ground precluded any major offensive maneuver from late December to early February. NARA

U.S. Army engineers repair the side of a road, partially washed out from the January rains, through Bir Mrabott in central Tunisia. Bir Mrabott is roughly 20 miles southeast of Gafsa on the Gabès road and was a proposed site for a mechanized attack by elements of II Corps' 1st Armored Division; however, it was called off when Gen. Lloyd Fredendall had decided to go on to the defensive in early February 1943. NARA

Tunisian mud was one of the worst enemies of the Allied advance on Tunis after the successful Operation Torch landings. Here a GI wears rubber galoshes, or waterproof overshoes. Despite these galoshes, movement would still be nightmarish for an infantryman with these ground conditions. NARA

North African Bedouins, or nomads, walk behind their camel in tank tread tracks made in the softened sand. An Allied vehicle is in the background, and behind it is a railway line constructed through the valley. NARA

American soldiers stand guard over French railroad workers and a halted train before the armistice with Vichy took effect three days after the amphibious landings. These GIs were part of the Center Task Force converging on Oran as the train was stopped near St. Leu. USAMHI

American soldiers lie prone on the valley floor in the Kasserine Pass, which is composed of sand, small rocks, and scrub. There was little cover for infantry to evade artillery or tank gun fire as well as fighter-bomber strafing runs. NARA

American soldiers have left their jeeps during an Axis artillery barrage and have sought cover on the reverse side of a small mound. NARA

On October 30, 1942, one week into Montgomery's Alamein offensive, soldiers of the Australian 2/3rd Pioneer Battalion take up position on a railway embankment, with the enemy holding the high ground on three sides, exposing the "diggers" to hazardous gun and artillery fire. These Australians were part of Monty's "crumbling" tactic, in which the Australian Imperial Force (AIF) 9th Division, utilizing their élan and offensive-mindedness, would advance through Axis infantry positions to the coastal road in the northern part of the line of attack. AWM

AIF 9th Division infantrymen at Tobruk during the spring of 1941 man a defensive position in stone sangars on the front line since the hardness of the ground precluded deep trenches. AWM

American soldiers in a slit trench roughly 25 miles from Mateur, just to the south of Bizerte. The GI on the right is firing his M1 Garand semiautomatic rifle, while it would appear that the soldier in the background is using a .303-inch caliber Bren light machine gun, based on the curved, top-loading magazine. NARA

Two British soldiers take cover behind a breastwork of rocks on a slight mound as a forward observation post to watch for an enemy mechanized column in the flat desert terrain. AUTHOR'S COLLECTION

An American soldier uses his shovel to fill sandbags with the dry desert soil from the slit trench that he has dug, in order to have some protection from Axis artillery and tank fire as well as strafing gunfire from an enemy airplane. NARA

A slight rise in the desert floor, with Tunisian mountains in the background, serves as a warren of slit trenches for American infantrymen. The terrain in central Tunisia comprised flat, rocky desert intermittently punctuated by the peaks of the Dorsal Mountains. NARA

A closer view of the slit trench position held by American infantry at El Guettar as soldiers march away to take up a new post. Combined arms combat between elements of the American II Corps and the 10th Panzer Division occurred at this central Tunisian desert locale between Gafsa and Sened on March 23, 1943. NARA

As a jeep leaves for a probable reconnaissance mission down a Tunisian road demarcated on either side by fence, American infantrymen manning a security position in protective slit trenches on the desert floor look on. In the background are the Tunisian Dorsal Mountains. NARA

Two American infantrymen stare out across an open expanse at an enemy position from their relatively deeply dug foxhole, covered with some rocks and straw around its edges to provide some basic camouflage. NARA

To maximize the effect of concentrated American artillery fire on a given target, forward observation posts like this one were necessary to redirect shellfire for accuracy. In this shallow entrenchment are two observers with binoculars and range finders, the latter manned by a captain, and two soldiers with telephones to connect them back to the artillery batteries in the rear. NARA

At the Battle of El Guettar, in late March 1943, between elements of Patton's II Corps and the German 10th Panzer Division, a forward artillery observer in his foxhole has a proximate view of American artillery rounds landing on the desert floor as the German tanks attempt to outflank the U.S. 1st Armored Division tanks and self-propelled artillery. USAMHI

An Australian in the open Western Desert near Bardia constructs his own improvised air raid shelter from frequent Italian Air Force bombing sorties. The exterior of his dugout is rimmed with parts from an Italian airplane wreck. AWM

An American U.S. Army Air Forces sergeant covered his foxhole with tin cans and other pieces of metal at an airfield at Youks-les-Bains, Algeria, roughly 12 miles northwest of Tebessa, as makeshift protection from Axis air raids. NARA

An American pilot climbs into his metal-reinforced foxhole during an air raid on his Algerian airfield. The metal might provide some protection from exploding shrapnel above and to the sides of his dugout. NARA

A cave in the Western Desert serves as a secluded command post obscured from enemy artillery spotters or aerial attack. AWM

At Tobruk in September 1941, a lonely Bren light machine gun team covers an Australian patrol from atop its rocky perch. AWM

British infantrymen of the 7th Rifle Brigade, part of the 7th Motor Brigade of the X Corps' 1st Armored Division in the Eighth Army, take cover behind the ruins of a Tunisian house from which Axis soldiers were recently driven in the Kounine Hills near Sousse in early May 1943. The soldier in the center hold his .303-inch caliber Bren light machine gun, while the others aim their .303-inch caliber Short Magazine Lee-Enfield (SMLE) bolt-action rifles. NARA

British soldiers use the window of a shell-and-bullet-riddled, ruined house in Tunisia as cover as Montgomery's Eighth Army advances from the south toward Sousse. The soldier on the left is firing an M1928 Thompson submachine gun. AUTHOR'S COLLECTION

An American soldier displays a new baggage carrier worn by his mule. In the mountainous and heavy scrub terrain of northern Tunisia, the use of mules became important for local off-road transport of supplies, wounded, and the dead. USAMHI

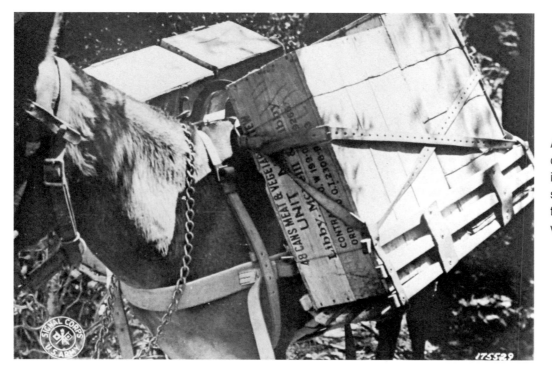

A mule laden with boxes of tinned rations is utilized in the thick Tunisian scrub country over tracks that would not support vehicles. USAMHI

A dead American soldier is brought back draped over a mule through a narrow trail with dense scrub on either side in northern Tunisia. USAMHI

When mules were unavailable for transport of supplies along impassable Tunisian scrub tracks, soldiers did the carrying. Here a group of American soldiers carry fuel cans and other items to the front. USAMHI

American engineers and British soldiers put the finishing touches to a wooden pontoon bridge that they erected across a waterway on the Bizerte-Tunis road. Shallow-draft pontoon boats are clearly visible under the wooden planking. AUTHOR'S COLLECTION

American engineers string cable for communications as M4 medium Sherman tanks of the 1st Armored Division move forward along the Tunisian desert floor in the Bir Mrabott Pass during fighting southeast of El Guettar. In the background is a typical Tunisian djebel, which refers to a hill or range of hills in North Africa. These local heights became important defensive positions in many battles for both sides. NARA

An American engineer using a magnetic mine detector sweeps the junction of a Tunisian road and adjacent desert. The retreating Axis forces commonly placed antipersonnel mines at locations such as these since Allied infantrymen would frequently be marching in column there to the side of the road surface. NARA

American combat engineers using visual inspection and prodding of the ground with a long bayonet where buried mines were suspected to try to clear the railway station at Kasserine in late February 1943 as part of II Corps' counteroffensive after the stinging Axis defeats just several days before. The signs denoting the location of this site have been covered up by military censors in this photograph. NARA

American combat engineers led by a lieutenant (middle) have uncovered a mine (right foreground) after probing the ground with a long bayonet. The soldier to the left is holding an M1928 Thompson submachine gun. NARA

An American combat engineer gently uncovers a German antipersonnel mine left during the Axis withdrawal from Kasserine on February 26, 1943. Rommel's retreating forces left more than 40,000 mines sown to delay the counteroffensive of II Corps after their recent setbacks. NARA

The North African terrain infrequently offered sites for concealment of artillery pieces; however, near this roadside and railway line, with Algerian djebels in the background, the crew of an American 37mm AT gun lie in wait. The setting is Les Andalouses, to the west of Oran, on November 15, 1942, just one week after the amphibious landing of the U.S. 26th Regimental Combat Team as part of the Center Task Force. USAMHI

An American 37mm AT gun crew have concealed and camouflaged their weapon in some dense Tunisian scrub. This gun was ineffective against the frontal armor of German panzers employed in North Africa. Since the Gazala battle, the British Eighth Army had been employing its very effective 6-pounder or 57mm AT gun, which the U.S. Army would be soon getting off of American factory production lines. NARA

Americans inspect a captured *Wehrmacht* PaK 40 75mm AT gun near Gafsa in February 1943. This gun, which initially saw combat in Tunisia, was much more effective than its American counterpart, the near-obsolete 37mm AT gun. USAMHI

An American truck column on the Tunisian desert floor, with surrounding hills in the background, spreads camouflage netting over their vehicles to help conceal them from Axis aircraft while they are idle on the open terrain. NARA

In Algeria, American engineers spread camouflage netting over stacks of ammunition crates on November 15, 1943. The Axis air attacks on both Allied shipping and ground targets were fierce, with better airfields both in Tunisia and on Sicily. USAMHI

An Allied artillery ammunition dump camouflaged with netting near an Algerian farm field. The netting is covered with burlap or "hessian" strips, which are woven pieces of fabric made from several vegetable fibers to make rope. This ammunition dump was concealed at Les Andalouses, west of Oran, one week after the amphibious landings of the Center Task Force. USAMHI

Canisters of American 105mm artillery shells are neatly stacked under olive trees as natural vegetation cover to serve as camouflage from enemy aircraft at Sbiba on the Sbeitla-Le Kef Road in central Tunisia. NARA

A relatively flat expanse of northern Tunisian land near Tunis housed a major Axis airfield, which from drainage and visibility standpoints was more suitable for combat sorties than were Allied counterparts in Algeria during the first several weeks after the invasion. Here the Axis air complex shows the effects of heavy Allied aerial bombardment, as the drier weather in March 1943 allowed for more American and British bombing missions. NARA

An American B-25 Mitchell bomber sits idle at a forward, rudimentary Algerian airfield during a sandstorm. Conditions such as these resulted in fewer Allied sorties against Axis targets and enabled a greater enemy air presence during the initial months after the invasion. NARA

A U.S. Navy Scout Bomber Douglas (SBD) Dauntless dive-bomber uses an Algerian road as a runway. The U.S. Navy planes were part of the carrier escort, which included the USS Ranger for the Western Task Force, until Twelfth Air Force squadrons could be flown in to Algerian airfields from Gibraltar. NARA

A typical village street in El Guettar, on the Gafsa-Gabès Road. The surrounding locale of El Guettar was the site of elements of U.S. II Corps repelling an attack by the German 10th Panzer Division on March 22–23, 1943. NARA

Artillery-scarred shells of former buildings in the Tunisian port city of Bizerte were evident as the Allies, notably the U.S. 9th Infantry Division and supporting armor of II Corps, closed in. USAMHI

Infantrymen of the U.S. 9th Infantry Division walk down tree-lined streets of Bizerte with their bayonets fixed as they combat sporadic sniper fire. After fighting in the northern Tunisian hills, this type of urban fighting was unusual and would prompt mock urban combat training for reinforcements as they arrived in North Africa. USAMHI

A pair of U.S. 9th Infantry Division soldiers hold their M1 Garand semiautomatic rifles at the ready as they visually inspect an upper floor of a ruined Bizerte building. M3 medium Lee tanks were employed with infantry teams and would use their machine guns and 37mm turret gun to neutralize snipers located by the infantrymen amid the building ruins. USAMHI

CHAPTER 3
COMMANDERS AND COMBATANTS

As alluded to in Chapter 1, British prime Minister Winston S. Churchill agreed to support the Marshall-Eisenhower plan for a major cross-Channel attack in 1943 or 1944 in order to secure President Franklin D. Roosevelt's support to commit American troops for the Northwest Africa invasion in late 1942. However, the Combined Chiefs of Staff needed to select a leader for commander in chief, Allied Forces. Gen. Dwight D. Eisenhower, who had no experience as a field commander, had been appointed as commander of American forces in Europe in June 1942 by his mentor, U.S. Army Chief of Staff Gen. George C. Marshall, after the former had served in the War Plans Division during the early months of the war. Some have contended that Eisenhower was appointed to lead the Allied Expeditionary Force in North Africa as a concession to the Americans by Churchill since the prime minister's military assistant, Brig. Ian Jacob, had penned in his diary, "the U.S. regarded the Mediterranean as a kind of dark hole into which one entered at one's own peril." In fact, after Marshall had appointed Eisenhower as the deputy Allied commander in charge of planning Operation Torch in late July 1942, it was understood by both the Army chief of staff and his naval counterpart, Adm. Ernest J. King, that they would both back his appointment to thereafter command the entire operation.

Once the decision was made to invade Northwest Africa in early November 1942, the command for Operation Torch was finalized to include Maj. Gen. George S. Patton Jr. to direct the landings and subsequent operations of the Western Task Force. Patton's principal goal would be to capture Casablanca on French Morocco's Atlantic coast after assaulting other landing areas at Safi 140 miles to the south, where his armored force would land; and Mehdia, 80 miles to the north and seaward of Port Lyautey, where the capture of two airfields at Port Lyautey and Sale would be targets. Allied land-based air support would be composed of both American and British squadrons, with Brig. Gen. James H. Doolittle (of recent Tokyo Raid fame) commanding the former, and once airfields ashore were secured would be designated as the Twelfth Air Force. Most of

Patton's infantry would land at Fedala, 12 miles north of Casablanca. These three forces, with air and naval support, would converge westward on Casablanca after swinging around to the east side of the city since there were an estimated 50,000 Vichy French troops in the city who might resist, thereby prohibiting a direct assault there.

Western Task Force, under Patton, would have two infantry divisions, one armored division, and two separate tank battalions, all totaling just under 35,000 American troops. To attack Safi, Maj. Gen. Ernest Harmon, the 2nd Armored Division commander, would also be in charge of a sub–task force, code-named Blackstone, which consisted of the 47th Infantry Regiment, 9th Infantry Division, two reinforced battalions of the 67th Armored Regiment, 2nd Armored Division, elements of the 70th Tank Battalion, and several artillery batteries. Blackstone's sub–task force contained 6,500 troops, including support units.

About 220 miles north of Safi, along the Moroccan coast, a component of the Western Task Force would land three amphibious groups at five beaches along 10 miles of shore to seize the Mehdia–Port Lyautey area, thereby establishing the northern flank of Western Task Force and capturing the two French airdromes. Port Lyautey lay 5 miles inland of Mehdia on the Sebou River. This would be called Sub–Task Force Goalpost, under the command of Maj. Gen. Lucian K. Truscott, and would comprise the 60th Infantry Regiment of the 9th Infantry Division, the 1st Battalion of the 66th Armored Regiment of the 2nd Armored Division, and elements of the 70th Tank Battalion (unattached), all totaling just over 9,000 men.

About 70 miles to the south of Mehdia, the Western Task Force's largest component disembarked the 3rd Infantry Division with some armor to seize the coastal town of Fedala and silence French coast batteries there, prior to moving 12 miles south toward Casablanca as part of the converging operation to envelop this latter major port from the landward side. This was code-named Sub–Task Force Brushwood, under the command of Maj. Gen. Jonathan W. Anderson. His force was made up of three regimental landing groups (RLGs) of the 7th, 15th, and 30th Infantry Regiments of the 3rd Infantry Division. In addition to the infantry, there were elements of the 2nd Armored Division that included the 1st Battalion of the 67th Armored Regiment and the 82nd Reconnaissance Battalion. Brushwood, with its support units, had more than 19,000 officers and men for the three RLGs.

Western Task Force's naval support would consist of one aircraft carrier, four escort carriers, three battleships, seven cruisers, and thirty-eight destroyers, all in addition to troop and cargo vessels. The naval task force would be under the command of Rear Adm. H. Kent Hewitt. Prior to the establishment of a land-based air presence, naval air support would be provided for the landing phase.

The Center Task Force would be led by Maj. Gen. Lloyd R. Fredendall, with landings at three beaches (X, Y, and Z) along a 50-mile stretch of Mediterranean coastline to the east and west of Oran, the Algerian city of 200,000 that was targeted for seizure. A dedicated team of 400 men from the 6th Armored Infantry Regiment of the U.S. 1st Armored Division would assault Oran harbor, Operation Reservist, to prevent sabotage to the port's facilities. The Center Task Force would include the U.S. 1st Infantry Division ("Big Red One") with the 1st Ranger Battalion attached to Combat Command B of the 1st Armored Division. Various artillery and engineer units would support the U.S. 1st Infantry Division and the 1st Ranger Battalion that were to land astride Oran, bringing the total strength of Fredendall's force to 25,000 men. Once ashore, Center Task Force's troops would converge 10 miles inland of Oran, after seizing roads, villages (such as Arzew, St. Leu, and St. Cloud), and two local airfields (Tafaraoui and La Senia), and then attack the city from three sides. A failed paratroop assault to assist in the seizure of two airfields near Oran was conducted by the American 2nd Battalion, 509th Parachute Infantry Regiment.

More than 200 miles to Oran's east, the Eastern Task Force disembarked assault troops off the coast of Algiers. This task force had the fewest American units available and would thus be composed of mostly British troops. In addition to the British dominating the naval and air support contingents, this Algiers-bound force had 23,000 of its total of 33,000 troops drawn from British and Commonwealth units. The U.S. Army would provide 10,000 soldiers comprising the 39th Regimental Combat Team (RCT) of the 9th Infantry Division along with the 168th RCT and the

3rd Battalion of the 135th Infantry Regiment, both from the 34th Infantry Division. The British units included the 6th British Commando Unit along with the 11th Brigade of the British 78th Division. All of the above-mentioned units in the initial landing would be under the command of U.S. Army major general Charles W. Ryder to mollify the Vichy French hostility toward the British, which had been aroused after the sinking of a number of French surface ships in North African ports to keep them out of Axis hands (killing many French sailors in the process). The Allied Combined Chiefs of Staff aimed to have an American "flavor" to this operation.

Eventually British lieutenant general Kenneth A.N. Anderson would lead Eastern Task Force into Algiers after a successful amphibious assault on either side of that Vichy French colonial administrative center. Later it would be redesignated British First Army of Anglo-American composition. The task for the British First Army was then to race 500 miles to the east and capture the port of Tunis, thereby preventing it from falling into German hands, as well as to control the rest of Tunisia as Gen. Bernard Montgomery's Eighth Army advanced from the east.

The Vichy French land forces in Northwest Africa comprised 55,000 troops in Morocco, 50,000 in Algeria, and 15,000 in Tunisia. These troops were mainly native colonial infantry units led by French officers. In addition, there were some French Foreign Legion units as well as Zouaves. However, despite these numbers, Vichy French equipment and armor were obsolete. As a result of the armistice of June 1940, Germany denied the French in North Africa any modern medium or heavy artillery or antitank (AT) or antiaircraft (AA) guns; however, twelve units of motorized field artillery were allowed to be maintained. Mechanized cavalry in Morocco, Algeria, and Tunisia had roughly 250 obsolete tanks and 160 armored cars. At Casablanca there were several destroyers, a cruiser with 6-inch guns, and the new battleship *Jean Bart*, which was incompletely constructed but capable of firing its 15-inch gun turrets. At Oran there were only destroyers and smaller craft.

Of the five "first-class" airfields in French Morocco, only the one at Port Lyautey, shielded by the winding Sebou River, had concrete runways; hence it was a primary Allied target. There were primary and secondary airfields in Algeria, both along the coast near Oran (such as La Senia) and Algiers (Maison Blanche) as well as inland, such as at Tafaraoui, 16 miles southeast of Oran. Primary airfields in Tunisia were located near Bizerte (Sidi Ahmed) and Tunis (El Aouina), with secondary ones at Kairouan and Gabès. Most of the Vichy French air presence would be in Morocco, with more than 150 planes manned by capable pilots, and along the Mediterranean coast, with roughly another 200 aircraft that could be drawn from inland fields. Some of the French fighters, such as the Dewoitine 520, were actually more maneuverable than Allied carrier-borne Navy fighters.

With the armistice signed between Adm. François Darlan and the Allies, former Vichy French forces were amalgamated from troops in Morocco and Algeria to provide a French military presence in Tunisia. Initially French forces, now fighting with the Allies, were to cover the two Dorsal mountain ranges to protect the British First Army flank as well as hinder any Axis attempt to enter Algeria from central Tunisia. The troops from Algeria and Morocco would aid in forming Gen. Louis-Marie Koeltz's XIX Army Corps. In addition to French troops, a variety of French colonial and French Foreign Legion units participated in the Allied effort. Many of these formations would require rearming and training to adequately combat the Axis troops.

In the early 1940s the *Wehrmacht* was the best army in the world. It excelled in small-scale action that focused on the importance of the infantryman's initiative and swift counterattack to reseize lost territory. As Eric Larrabee points out, "no one who ever met a panzer division in full cry wanted to repeat the encounter." Especially after the heavy losses in Libya, the Italian troops displayed all the handicaps of an impoverished nation attempting to field a modern army. Field Marshal Albert Kesselring, the Axis commander in chief, South, in Rome, complained that Italian infantry was antiquated, having been based on colonial tactical doctrine. Some units, notably the specialized Bersaglieri and the Young Fascists, were good combat troops. Italian armor was also inadequate, with thin armor and inadequate turret guns to suitably combat the Allied tanks; however, many units were highly regarded by the Germans, to the extent that they were incorporated into German panzer formations rather than simply reinforcing Italian infantry. Italian artillery was deemed adequate, largely because of the reputed élan of its artillery crews, but many of the field piece types were still relatively obsolete. Steven Zaloga has commented, "The performance of Italian troops in Tunisia was undoubtedly far better than in Egypt in 1940 or in the Libyan campaign of 1941, but the Italian army remained a weak link in the Axis coalition."

On November 17, about 45 miles to the west of Bizerte, Allied troops would encounter their first Axis opposition. The closest Anderson's First Army would get to Tunis would be approximately 15 miles by the end of November 1942. Eisenhower's fear of Axis reinforcement of Tunisia with sizable reinforcement and against no French opposition had become a reality as Axis units were airlifted into Tunisia. The Allies were to meet the German 5th Panzer Army, which had reinforced the Tunisian bridgehead. It comprised the German *Korpsgruppe Fischer* and the Italian XXX Corps. There were also some specialty Axis infantry units including an ad hoc one formed from *Luftwaffe* paratroops as well as the Italian 10th Bersaglieri Regiment. Other Axis units to arrive later, to become part of Gen. Hans-Jürgen von Arnim's 5th Panzer Army, included the German 334th Infantry Division along with the 10th and 21st Panzer Divisions. Battles in Tunisia would witness the debut of the German Mk VI "Tiger" tank. By late January, von Arnim's forces in the Tunisian bridgehead would include 74,000 German and 26,000 Italian troops. German air support in Tunisia was an advantage that the Axis forces possessed over the Allies. This was based on Sicily and southern Italy's proximity to the battle zone, and well-developed airbases and facilities there.

As Field Marshal Erwin Rommel retreated westward into Tunisia from Montgomery's Eighth Army, his defeated El Alamein veteran 15th Panzer as well as 90th and 164th Light Divisions would be added to the Axis strength by January 1943; however, several units would be transferred to von Arnim's command in central Tunisia for refitting away from the Eighth Army's advance. Rommel's German contingent of *Panzer-Armee Afrika* would number roughly 30,000 troops among understrength battle groups, while the Italian infantry and armored divisions comprised 48,000 troops. After the losses at both battles of El Alamein and Alam Halfa, Rommel possessed only about 130 German and Italian tanks, of which only 60 were fully operational, and among those half were Italian obsolete models. The fortunes of war in the North African desert would now allow the two main Axis forces in that theater to form the Tunisian defense to the Allied pincer moving east and north into Tunisia.

Hitler intended to raise Nazi strength in the Tunisian bridgehead to 140,000 troops; however, his drive for Stalingrad would ultimately limit the reinforcements sent to North Africa. Nonetheless, from November 1942 through January 1943, more than 80,000 German and 30,000 Italian troops would be shipped or airlifted into Tunisia, along with more than 400 tanks and 700 artillery pieces. As the Allies were to establish themselves after the landings in Northwest Africa, Axis supplies to the Tunisian bridgehead, which peaked in January 1943, began to decline steadily thereafter, contributing to enemy shortages of all types of war matériel.

Field Marshal Albert Kesselring, a *Luftwaffe* officer, was appointed C-in-C South in December 1941, with his headquarters based near Rome. Prior to that Kesselring helped create the operational mechanics of the *Luftwaffe*; commanded Hitler's air squadrons in the Mediterranean theater; and reported to the Italian Fascist leader, Benito Mussolini, as well. Having combat experience in both Poland and France, he was instrumental in the development of tactical aerial assault, notably with his squadrons of Ju 87 (*Stuka*) dive-bombers in 1939 and 1940, which he brought to the Mediterranean theater along the North African littoral. NARA

Field Marshal Erwin Rommel stands victoriously in his staff car, wearing his iconic desert military uniform and accoutrements, with his 15th Panzer Division in the Cyrenaican desert between Tobruk and Sidi Omar, the latter near the Egyptian frontier, in late 1941. Rommel was a decorated WWI veteran and during the interwar years a military author, having written *Infantry Attacks*. After commanding Hitler's bodyguard in Poland, he was awarded with the *Wehrmacht*'s 7th Panzer Division, which won much acclaim for its dash across northern France in May 1940. In February 1941 he was sent to Libya at the head of the nascent *Deutsches Afrikakorps* (DAK), which was to achieve almost mythical fame destroying the reputations of several British generals until his push to Egypt and the Suez Canal was stopped, first by Claude Auchinleck in July 1942, and then by Montgomery in August 1942 at Alam Halfa. It was Montgomery's offensive and ultimate victory at Second Alamein in October and November 1942 that forced Rommel to retreat with his *Panzer-Armee Afrika* across Libya into southern Tunisia, where he was to gain renown again in his offensive through the Kasserine Pass in late February 1943 against elements of the U.S. II Corps and the British First Army. NARA

Gen. Hans-Jürgen von Arnim, on May 15, 1943, marches into captivity, just days after surrendering the Axis forces in North Africa. Von Arnim was a highly decorated *Wehrmacht* officer, having served in Poland, France, and Russia. Although having a fractious relationship with both Rommel and Kesselring, by not obeying orders to support Rommel in operations west of the Kasserine Pass in late February 1943, he successfully led elements of his 5th Panzer Army on an offensive through the Faïd Pass and then inflicted heavy casualties on U.S. II Corps units at Sidi Bou Zid on February 14, 1943. NARA

Italian general Maresciallo Giovanni Messe (right), commander of the Italian First Army, with German general Kurt von Liebenstein (left), stand together. During the Tunisian campaign, von Arnim was given command of Army Group Africa. Rommel's former command of the *Panzer-Armee Afrika* or remnants of the German-Italian Army fighting in southern Tunisia was taken over by Messe, who had battle experience in Ethiopia, Albania, Greece, and Russia. AUTHOR'S COLLECTION

Gen. Wilhelm Ritter von Thoma (left), in his combat uniform, at an informal meeting with Gen. Bernard Montgomery (wearing pullover at right) at Eighth Army desert headquarters after the former's capture by the 11th Hussars in one of the final tank actions of the Second Battle of El Alamein on November 4, 1942. Prior to North Africa, von Thoma was considered a specialist in mechanized force tactics, having commanded both the 6th and 20th Panzer Divisions in Russia. Interestingly, in October 1940, von Thoma was sent to North Africa to assess whether the *Wehrmacht* should assist the Italians in driving the British out of Egypt. He advocated sending four panzer divisions to North Africa, which was twice the number eventually dispatched to Tripoli to aid the faltering Italians after their rout at Beda Fomm in early February 1941. Von Thoma took over the DAK, under Rommel's overall *Panzer-Armee Afrika* command, after Gen. Walther Nehring was wounded at Alam Halfa in August 1942. When Rommel was evacuated to Germany in late September 1942 to restore his health, Gen. Georg Stumme arrived from Russia to take over for Rommel, but he died of a heart attack at the onset of Second Alamein after his staff car drove into an Australian patrol. The *Panzer-Armee Afrika* was briefly leaderless, until von Thoma took it over pending Rommel's return to the battlefield. The DAK command then reverted back to von Thoma. NARA

Gen. Sir Alan Brooke (right), chief, Imperial General Staff (CIGS), in Egypt in August 1942 speaking with Brig. Eric "Chink" Dorman-Smith, who was Auchinleck's de facto deputy. Dorman-Smith, like Auchinleck, was unceremoniously sacked by Churchill and Brooke in the "August Purge" despite the halting of Rommel's forces during the combat that comprised the First Battle of El Alamein. Dorman-Smith was also influential in the success of Operation Compass in December 1940, as it was his idea to attack the Italian fortified camps from the rear when he observed aerial photographs showing numerous tracks from Italian trucks supplying the camps, which indicated that there were no minefields there. Operation Torch was the idea of Brooke and Churchill, who then successfully sought to win over Roosevelt to the invasion of Northwest Africa. Another leg to the Churchill-Brooke journey was to visit the Russians and explain to Stalin why the Allies could not invade France in 1942 and would instead attack in Northwest Africa. Brooke became a field marshal in January 1944. AUTHOR'S COLLECTION

British prime minister Winston Churchill (right) addresses a gathering of British troops, with Secretary for War Anthony Eden (left) and Lt. Gen. Kenneth A.N. Anderson (center). Anderson was appointed to command the British First Army after mostly American forces from the Eastern Task Force landed at beaches around Algiers. Anderson, who had a reputation for being extremely taciturn, would be charged with racing his First Army across Algeria and northern Tunisia in an attempt to reach Tunis and Bizerte in December 1942 before Axis forces could reinforce those bridgeheads. AWM

Gen. Dwight D. Eisenhower, the C-in-C of Allied Forces in North Africa, with his trademark smile. The photograph was taken in Algiers in early 1943 after the assassination of French admiral Darlan. Although a successful armistice was concluded on November 22, 1942, Eisenhower had to weather a political firestorm with accusations that he was working with a Nazi collaborator. NARA

Britain's senior commanders in North Africa in 1942–43. From left to right stand Senior Air Staff Officer (SASO) Harry Broadhurst, Air Vice Marshal (AVM) Arthur Coningham, Gen. Bernard L. Montgomery, Gen. Sir Harold Alexander, and Air Officer Commanding, Middle East, Arthur Tedder. Broadhurst was a Royal Air Force (RAF) fighter pilot and squadron commander who specialized in close support between ground and air forces. In the Middle East in late 1942, he was the SASO to AVM Coningham, then the commander of the Desert Air Force (DAF). The two quarreled over the objectives of the DAF, with Broadhurst eventually getting the command of this unit as the youngest AVM in the RAF and improving the role of ground support fighter-bombers in interdicting Axis transport and lines of communication across North Africa. Coningham, a native Australian who served with the New Zealand Expeditionary Force in WWI and subsequently the Royal Flying Corps (later the RAF), was influential in the development of forward air control parties. After commanding the DAF from 1941–1943, he was promoted as the commander of Tactical Air Forces for the Normandy campaign. Montgomery, as the leader of the Eighth Army, praised Broadhurst for the RAF support of his troops moving westward after the victory at El Alamein in November 1942. Alexander, who was the C-in-C Middle East succeeding Auchinleck in August 1942, would eventually lead the Allied 18th Army Group Headquarters in Tunisia beginning in February 1943, essentially serving as Eisenhower's deputy. Tedder, born in Scotland, played pivotal roles in 1941 with the evacuation of Crete and during Operation Crusader, the latter breaking the siege of Tobruk. Tedder would take over the Mediterranean Air Command for the invasions of Sicily and Italy before becoming the deputy supreme commander at Supreme Headquarters Allied Expeditionary Force (SHAEF) under Eisenhower for the Normandy invasion. NARA

Lieutenant General Eisenhower reviews Royal Marines in front of a British warship in Britain during the summer of 1942. On June 11, 1942, Marshall inquired whether Eisenhower's plans for Operation Torch were complete, since the Army chief of staff had decided to have Eisenhower command all American forces in Britain in prelude to the invasion of Northwest Africa, just a few months away, when he would become supreme commander for the Mediterranean theater. Some saw Eisenhower's command for the North African invasion as a political concession to General Marshall, who was resistant to Churchill's plans for Operation Torch. NARA

General Eisenhower (left), upon leaving for England in mid-1942, was able to choose a deputy. His choice was Maj. Gen. Mark Clark (center), who worked with Eisenhower on Marshall's staff in Washington after the war's outbreak. At the far right is Rear Adm. H. Kent Hewitt, who would command Task Force 34, the Western Task Force that would land Patton's troops along Morocco's Atlantic coast. NARA

Vichy French admiral Darlan (left) and recently promoted American lieutenant general Mark Clark shake hands after signing a formal armistice in Algiers on November 22, 1942. Darlan was C-in-C of the Vichy armed forces, the prime minister to Vichy president Henri Philippe Pétain, and the designated successor to him as well. Eisenhower sent Clark on November 9 to Algiers to broker a ceasefire. The American envoy to the Vichy French in North Africa, Robert Murphy, was to assist in the negotiations. Within twenty-four hours a deal was struck to include a general ceasefire, with Darlan becoming the de facto military governor of North Africa. The Vichy government was informed, and the Germans immediately seized the unoccupied zone of France. Eisenhower endorsed the Clark-Darlan deal when he arrived in Algiers on November 13. Both Washington and London erupted in criticism, somewhat hypocritically, over the deal, largely due to Darlan's odious reputation. Nonetheless an armistice ensued; however, Darlan was assassinated. NARA

French general Henri Giraud (left) meets with President Franklin Roosevelt (right) and Harry Hopkins (standing), an advisor, emissary, and general political factotum to Roosevelt, in Casablanca in early 1943. Giraud was initially courted by the Americans under the belief that the French military in North Africa would devote themselves to him and not Gen. Charles de Gaulle, leader of Free French forces based in London. Giraud was a WWI veteran and commanded the French Ninth Army in 1940 until his capture. He was interned until 1942 and escaped to unoccupied France. Ultimately most of the senior French military officers in North Africa refused to accept the prospect of him as their leader. After the assassination of Darlan, command of the French North African garrison, following their decision to side with the Allies, went to General Giraud, with French forces reporting directly to Maj. Gen. Lucian Truscott, acting as Eisenhower's deputy chief of staff for Tunisian operations. NARA

Lt. Gen. George S. Patton stares forward in an iconic pose shortly after getting his third star in March 1943. Patton led the Western Task Force that landed along the Atlantic coast of Morocco and captured Casablanca after heavy fighting around Mehdia and Port Lyautey. Patton, via envoys to French general Charles-Auguste-Paul Noguès in Casablanca, threatened to raze the city, and a ceasefire was arranged. He subsequently commanded the I Armored Corps in Morocco, which consisted of the 2nd Armored Division and a few separate tank battalions, until assuming command of the II Corps in central Tunisia after the debacle at Kasserine Pass in late February 1943. NARA

Maj. Gen. George S. Patton (left) and Rear Adm. H. Kent Hewitt, commander of Task Force 34, the Western Task Force, share a humorous moment aboard the cruiser flagship, USS *Augusta*, before the amphibious landing along the Atlantic coast of French Morocco. NARA

General Eisenhower (right) visiting with Maj. Gen. Patton on March 16, 1943, to go over his plans for the II Corps attack on Gafsa as part of a continuation of the late winter offensive in central Tunisia. Patton had assumed command of II Corps after its previous commander, Maj. Gen. Lloyd Fredendall, was sent home after the Axis offensives in February 1943 at both Sidi Bou Zid and Kasserine Pass, both resulting in excessive losses of American men and matériel. This visit was also an occasion to give Patton his third star and promote him to the rank of lieutenant general. NARA

Maj. Gen. Ernest N. Harmon bounds out of an airplane in Tunisia. Harmon led the 2nd Armored Division ashore at Fedala on D-Day and was sent by Eisenhower to Tunisia to assess what caused the defeat at Kasserine and Faïd Passes in February 1943. After submitting his report about the unnecessary casualties at Kasserine and Sidi Bou Zid, Harmon returned to Tunisia within six weeks to take over the command of the 1st Armored Division from Maj. Gen. Orlando Ward. Patton's recommendation to replace the well-liked Ward with the fearless and bullheaded Harmon was the correct one, as the American 1st Armored Division started to win battles. NARA

Lt. Gen. George Patton (left) goes over a communiqué with Maj. Gen. Hugh J. Gaffey, one of his trusted staff officers. Gaffey became Patton's deputy chief of staff after the Sicilian campaign when Maj. Gen. Geoffrey Keyes was promoted to command a corps. Gaffey had commanded the 2nd Armored Division in Sicily under Patton and had some misgivings about giving up a combat division for a staff position. NARA

Lt. Gen. George Patton (left) and Maj. Gen. Geoffrey Keyes (center), who was a capable deputy chief of staff for Patton, a confidant, and a fine trainer of men, stand among a gathering of French officers in Morocco. Keyes would command the 2nd Armored Division and would eventually be promoted to lead a corps after the Sicilian campaign ended. Here both stand among French officers in Morocco in March 1943. NARA

A triumvirate of Allied generals stand at attention and offer a salute. On the left is Gen. Sir Harold Alexander, commander of 18th Army Group in Tunisia. In the center is Lt. Gen. Mark Clark, who functioned as Eisenhower's "right arm" in North Africa and would go on to command the U.S. Fifth Army in Italy. On the right is Lt. Gen. Omar Bradley, a West Point classmate of Eisenhower's. Bradley was sent into Tunisia as an aide to Patton after the latter assumed command of the II Corps from Fredendall. He replaced Patton as commander of II Corps during the final month of fighting for Bizerte as Patton returned to Algiers for the Sicily campaign planning. NARA

General Eisenhower in the front passenger seat of a jeep with II Corps commander Lt. Gen. Omar Bradley in the rear, in Tunisia during the closing weeks of combat made fierce by the tenacity of the Germans in the rugged hill country near Bizerte. Bradley's plan to capture Bizerte was to first seize Mateur. He would utilize the U.S. 9th Infantry Division along the northern coast with the 1st and 34th Infantry Divisions in the hill country to the south. His 1st Armored Division would strike wherever a breakthrough in the tough Axis defenses was achieved. Eisenhower held his classmate Bradley in high esteem, respecting his tacit manner, in contrast to Patton's bluster, as a true merit. NARA

Maj. Gen. Lloyd R. Fredendall was perceived to be a "Marshall man" and was given the command of U.S. II Corps after he landed his assault troops of the Center Task Force to capture Oran after some hard fighting against the Vichy French. Here he decorates a war correspondent, Leo Disher, with a Purple Heart for multiple wounds sustained covering the combat in Oran Harbor on November 8, 1942. Fredendall was opinionated, Anglophobic, and had disdain for the new French allies. He was also one of the older corps commanders in the U.S. Army during the war. However, he is most remembered for the twin II Corps disasters that occurred on his watch at Sidi Bou Zid and Kasserine Pass in February 1943. The blame was placed squarely on his shoulders, and he was replaced at corps headquarters by Patton, with Bradley to provide assistance to him. NARA

Brig. Gen. Lucian K. Truscott Jr. commanded the Sub–Task Force Goalpost and was tasked with the capture the Mehdia–Port Lyautey area to secure the northern flank of the Western Task Force's assault on Morocco's Atlantic coast. After some hard fighting to achieve his objective, Eisenhower appointed the relatively junior Truscott to be his deputy chief of staff and representative for operations in Tunisia, with his headquarters in Constantine. After the Vichy armistice and amalgamation of French forces into the Allied Order of Battle, Eisenhower, through Truscott, would coordinate the parallel activities of the three national forces fighting the Axis in Tunisia. After the successful Tunisian campaign ended, Major General Truscott would lead the 3rd Infantry Division in the invasion of Sicily. NARA

During Operation Torch, Maj. Gen. Orlando "Pinky" Ward, shown here on the left, commanded the U.S. 1st Armored Division. He was meeting with Maj. Gen. Andrew Bruce, head of the Tank Destroyer Force, in late February 1943 in Tunisia. Ward's division trained for more than a year before going to Britain in the spring of 1942. The 1st Armored Division landed with the Center Task Force at Oran on November 8, 1942, and then moved into Tunisia. Ward had a fractious relationship with II Corps commander Fredendall, who had placed elements of the 1st Armored Division in specific locations with specific tasks assigned. During the Kasserine and Faïd battles, Fredendall had erred in his placement of 1st Armored Division units on isolated hills, which contributed to their encirclement and destruction. Because of Fredendall's "micromanagement," Ward was unable to respond with speed and freedom of maneuver to the crisis. Major General Harmon, commander of the U.S. 2nd Armored Division in Morocco, reviewed the Kasserine and Sidi Bou Zid battles for Eisenhower, noting that Ward's leadership was solid, but not Fredendall's, and recommended the latter's relief with Patton. USAMHI

Maj. Gen. Terry de la Mesa Allen (left, smoking cigarette), commanding general of the 1st U.S. Infantry Division, negotiates with a Vichy French officer (right) and Maj. William O. Darby, commander of the 1st Ranger Battalion (second from right), after some hard fighting in Oran after landings by the Center Task Force. Allen led a large contingent, comprising his 16th and 18th Regimental Combat Teams (RCTs), an armored task force, and the 1st Ranger Battalion, on to Oran from the hills above the Algerian village of St. Cloud to the east after landings at St. Leu and Arzew. Concurrent with this move the assistant division commander, Brig. Gen. Theodore Roosevelt Jr., led his 26th Infantry RCT toward Oran from the west, after landing at Les Andalouses. This pincer drove roughly 9,000 Vichy French soldiers into a 20-mile-diameter perimeter that had to be reduced. Allen was a commissioned officer veteran of WWI who was wounded at St. Mihiel in 1918, and after having had a checkered career at some of the Army staff colleges during the interwar years, he impressed Lt. Col. George C. Marshall at Fort Benning's Infantry School in 1932. Although he flunked out of West Point in his last year there, he was the first one in his original class to receive a brigadier general's star. NARA

Maj. William O. Darby, commander of the 1st Ranger Battalion, which assaulted French coastal forts at Arzew as part of the Center Task Force's operations to seize Oran. A West Point graduate who started soldiering as an officer in the Army's last horse artillery unit, he gained notoriety as a trainer of a specialized U.S. Army unit that was to be modeled on the British Commandos. Brigadier General Truscott, who oversaw the unit's training first in Northern Ireland and then in Scotland before the North African invasion, said of Darby, "Never in this war have I known a more gallant, heroic officer." In fact, it was Truscott who selected the name "Rangers" for this unit based on the pre–Revolutionary War colonial unit that went by the same name after being formed by Maj. Robert Rogers to fight alongside the British during the French and Indian War. NARA

Brig. Gen. Lucian K. Truscott Jr. (middle with officer's hat and cavalryman's boots) and Maj. William O. Darby (to the right of Truscott) review Darby's 1st Battalion Rangers in Achnacarry, Scotland, after a rigorous training period supervised by officers and NCOs of the British Commandos. Of the original 575 volunteers for this elite unit, roughly 20 percent were sent back to their original units. USAMHI

French general Louis-Marie Koeltz (left), who commanded the French XIX Corps in Tunisia, decorates Maj. Gen. Terry de la Mesa Allen (middle) and Brig. Gen. Theodore Roosevelt Jr. (right) with the *Croix de Guerre* award for their leadership of the U.S. 1st Infantry Division. Koeltz's corps was positioned between Anderson's British First Army and Fredendall's U.S. II Corps. NARA

Brig. Gen. Theodore Roosevelt Jr. after landing with his 26th RCT at Les Andalouses for a converging attack on Oran from the west. He was described as a "short, wrinkled figure clutching a riding crop … frequently wore shabby, tattered fatigues and a wool cap … he could have been taken for a battalion cook," as shown above. However, his career was dotted with brilliance, despite walking in the shadow of his larger-than-life presidential father, who, too, basked in the fame of combat at San Juan Hill with his U.S. Cavalry (Volunteers), the "Rough Riders." T.R.'s son, "Ted" Roosevelt, was a wealthy investment banker before serving as a battalion commander in his beloved 26th Infantry Regiment and was wounded in WWI, exiting the conflict as a lieutenant colonel. His private life postings during the interwar years are noteworthy for accomplishment, diversity, talent, and intellect, including assistant secretary of the Navy, governor general of Puerto Rico, colonial governor of the Philippines, chairman of American Express, and an officer of Doubleday Publishing. NARA

Maj. Gen. Charles W. Ryder, commanding general of the U.S. 34th Infantry Division, which amphibiously assaulted the beaches surrounding Algiers with other elements of the Eastern Task Force. Ryder was a West Point classmate of both Eisenhower and Bradley, who received numerous combat decorations during WWI. Both Darlan and his French Army counterpart, Gen. Alphonse Juin, realized that with fewer than 10,000 men Algiers would be forced to surrender to Ryder soon after the invasion. AUTHOR'S COLLECTION

Maj. Gen. James Doolittle, commanding general of U.S. Air Forces in North Africa, which would comprise the new Twelfth Air Force. Doolittle was a pioneer racing aviator before the war and had won the Medal of Honor for his Tokyo Raid on April 18, 1942. In North Africa he and his British counterparts were pitted against Allied ground commanders who wanted more support and interference with the numerous Axis sorties flown against them. Doolittle had to transition his rapid buildup of air assets in western Algeria to more forward airfields closer to the combat. Between Casablanca and the Tunisian border, there were only four hard-surfaced runways that were usable in the beginning of the campaign. Although sorties were being flown by the RAF's Eastern Air Command, supporting British First Army, and the U.S. Twelfth Air Force, they were aimed to rear echelon Axis landing grounds and ports. Only RAF Spitfires flying off Souk el Arba and U.S. P-38 Lightnings and A-20 Havocs from Youks-les-Bains gave the necessary front-line support to Anderson's First Army infantry in the drive for Tunis in November and December 1942. NARA

Maj. Gen. Manton S. Eddy, commanding general of the U.S. 9th Infantry Division, sits in his jeep with his assistant division commander, Brig. Gen. Daniel Stroh, in Bizerte at the conclusion of the conflict on May 8, 1943. Eddy was described as energetic and imaginative, but his troops during the March/April 1943 combat were scattered and ill-prepared to assault Axis fixed defenses. In May elements of his division along with M3 medium Lee tanks had to clear out Bizerte's Axis snipers with urban street fighting. NARA

Lt. Gen. George S. Patton (left) and Lt. Gen. Omar Bradley (center) meet with Maj. Gen. Matthew B. Ridgway, commanding general of the 82nd Airborne Division, at Oujda in French Morocco in June 1943 after the Tunisian campaign had ended. Paratroop missions in North Africa were few. The British suffered heavy losses when more than 500 paratroopers of the 1st Parachute Battalion, under the command of Lt. Col. John D. Frost, were dropped south of Tunis to wreak havoc on the Axis forces there. However, after being confronted by German panzers and losing almost 300 men, Frost retreated toward Medjez with the survivors of his battalion. The U.S. 509th Parachute Infantry Regiment, under Col. Edson Raff, after its unfortunate experience at Oran, was to be dropped without any opposition at Youks-les-Bains, near Tebessa, in mid-November. Raff's paratroopers also fought at Gafsa as Axis forces continued their buildup there at the end of November 1942. NARA

Robert Murphy (left), the American diplomat to Vichy France in North Africa, stands in Algiers with Gen. Alphonse Juin, commanding general of French ground forces in North Africa. Juin went on to become the French commander in Tunisia after the armistice was in place and Vichy French soldiers joined the Allied cause. However, he was primarily tasked with rebuilding the French Army in North Africa for later campaigns in Italy and France. NARA

Maj. Gen. George Patton (right) with French general Charles-Auguste-Paul Noguès, the resident-general for Morocco, in Rabat, French Morocco, after the armistice had been signed. At the time of the Moroccan assault by the Western Task Force, Noguès vacillated between cooperating with the Allies or Vichy until the ceasefire. On D-Day, ultimately, Noguès had decided to initially resist the invasion despite an aborted coup to overthrow the Vichy regime in Morocco; however, as the assault waves landed with accompanying Allied naval gunfire, the French resident-general negotiated a ceasefire with Patton's emissaries. NARA

Free French general Jacques-Philippe Leclerc (his nom de guerre) enjoys some levity with British tankers approaching the Mareth Line in 1943. Leclerc had his formal military training at St. Cyr and at the Cavalry School in Saumur. He fought against the Germans in 1939 but was captured. He eventually escaped to England, took the name Leclerc to shield his family from any reprisals, and joined de Gaulle's Free French forces. Leading Free French troops as a brigadier general in sub-Saharan Chad, he eventually linked up with the westward-moving British Eighth Army in Libya after El Alamein. He was promoted to major general in 1943. With Montgomery's forces Leclerc commanded "L" Force, composed of Free French and former French colonial troops. NARA

Lt. Gen. Sir Henry Maitland Wilson (left) and Maj. Gen. Bernard Freyberg, VC (right), in Greece in 1941. Wilson was instrumental as general officer commanding, Egypt, in the Operation Compass victories over the Italians in the Western Desert from late December 1941 to February 1943; however, he led a British and Commonwealth expedition to Greece that was disastrous, leading to evacuation after it was easily beaten by German forces there later in 1941. Freyberg, a New Zealander, commanded his country's forces in Greece and was then the overall commander on Crete, which likewise led to an evacuation and many captured. With Montgomery's Eighth Army, Freyberg commanded the New Zealand Corps in southern Tunisia, which comprised his 2nd New Zealand Division, the 8th Independent Armored Brigade, and Leclerc's "L" Force. AWM

American GIs of the Eastern Task Force hauling their equipment through the Algiers harbor after the ceasefire was declared. The soldiers are carrying extra bandoliers of ammunition as well as full musette bags or small knapsacks. USAMHI

The crew of an M3 medium Lee tank cooks a warm meal in the Tunisian desert, with their armored vehicle in profile. This tank was heavily armored and included two .30-inch caliber machine guns, one in the top turret and the other located adjacent to a 37mm turret gun. The sponson on the right side of the hull housed a 75mm M2 gun that could fire high-explosive, armor-piercing, and smoke rounds. The gun had major traverse limitations, but until the M4 medium Sherman tank became available, there was no conventional turret capable of housing the 75mm gun. This tank does not have a muzzle counterweight on its 75mm gun. The tank shown above had a crew of six, which included a commander, a 75mm gunner, a 37mm gunner, two assistant gunners, and a driver. USAMHI

A group of seven soldiers stand by their M3 half-track at a bivouac in the Tunisian desert. The M3 was widely used by all Allied forces, mainly as a personnel carrier such as shown above, but other variants existed, too. Production of the M3 began in earnest in 1941, with more than 40,000 produced that year. As an infantry carrier, it could have up to thirteen soldiers and could mount a variety of machine guns. The half-track above has a .50-inch caliber antiaircraft (AA) machine gun mounted in its rear. NARA

Two tankers from an American tank crew, with the middle one wounded, give an account of the conflict they encountered against the Vichy French defenders in Oran. USAMHI

Soldiers from the U.S. 1st Infantry Division in Oran go through some captured French weapons and items following some heavy fighting after amphibious forces from the Center Task Force converged on the Algerian port city from beaches to the east and west. NARA

American officers from the U.S. 1st Infantry Division take a well-deserved rest after fighting subsided with a ceasefire in the Algerian port city of Oran. USAMHI

American GIs strike a relaxed pose in some of the more rugged North African country before embarking into Axis-held territory after the initial port cities were captured during the initial phase of Operation Torch. NARA

An American soldier from the Eastern Task Force lights up a cigarette for a French seaman in Fedala on the Atlantic coast of Morocco. The French sailors and fleet put up a stout resistance to both the landing waves as well as ships offshore before Patton's staff arranged a ceasefire with French general Noguès after three days of bloody fighting. NARA

An American paratrooper, identified by his uniform, boots, and carbine, admires the medals of a Spahi, which refers to a light cavalryman recruited from the native populations of Morocco, Algeria, and Tunisia. When mounted and on parade, the Spahis would often sport flowing, long white capes. NARA

Staff officers of the all African-American 99th Fighter (Pursuit) Squadron stationed at Fez, Morocco, in May 1943. At the far left is Lt. Col. Benjamin O. Davis Jr., the squadron's commanding officer. Davis became the first African-American general officer in the U.S. Air Force, and in 1998 he received his fourth star. He followed in the footsteps of his father, Benjamin O. Davis Sr., who was the first African-American general in the U.S. Army. NARA

African-American soldiers of the 90th Coastal Artillery Corps man their 90mm AA gun in Casablanca, French Morocco. NARA

A coastal artillery sergeant blows his alarm whistle warning of approaching enemy planes so that gunners could get to their AA batteries. Early on, due to a dearth of airfields, the recently captured port cities as well as front-line troop dispositions were heavily bombed by Axis aircraft, until air parity could be achieved in the late winter of 1943. USAMHI

American litter-bearers carry one of their wounded comrades down a 6-mile trail through Tunisian scrub in late April 1943, when U.S. II Corps was fighting in the rugged hill country to get to Mateur and subsequently Bizerte. NARA

An M3 light Stuart tank. The M3 tank's large-scale manufacturing began in mid-1941 in an attempt to add more armor to the older M2 light tank. The M3 light tank was admired by British tankers, who utilized it under Lend-Lease, for its speed and reliability, winning the moniker "Honey." Unfortunately, when the light tanks of the U.S. 1st Armored Division engaged the *Wehrmacht*'s panzers in Tunisia, it was evident, as the British had also realized fighting Rommel, that the tank was underarmored and its 37mm main turret gun was ill-suited to take on the Panzers III and IV in North Africa. Due to these deficiencies, the M3 light tank was relegated mainly to reconnaissance and flank protection. AUTHOR'S COLLECTION

An M3 medium Lee tank in training at Fort Knox, Kentucky, in early 1942. This armored vehicle was hastily designed to augment the firing power of its predecessor, the M2 medium tank. Mass production began in August 1941 and continued until the end of December 1942. The British used the M3 medium tanks in North Africa in early 1942, as Allied partners, calling their tanks "Grants." Since the more powerful main 75mm gun was mounted in the sponson, it had a limited traverse and, thus, field of fire, while the 37mm gun in the main turret lacked the necessary firepower to combat German panzers. Also, the tank presented a very tall profile. Despite these disadvantages, the M3 Lee and Grant medium tanks served with distinction in Burma and in the Pacific after becoming obsolete in North Africa. LIBRARY OF CONGRESS

An M4A2 medium Sherman tank. This versatile Allied tank was designed to replace the M3 medium tank in mid-1940. To hasten the M4 tank's production, the chassis, tracks, bogey wheels, etc., were all the same as for the M3. The major improvement in the M4 lay in its 75mm gun housed in a turret, with a complete 360-degree traverse. The tank held a crew of five. Production commenced in early 1942 with the first complement that was to initially outfit American armored units going to the Middle East for Montgomery's El Alamein offensive. Numerous variants were created on the M4 prototype. Like its M3 predecessor, it had a high profile, but less pronounced. However, its range was 50 percent greater than that of either the M3 light or medium tank. Almost 50,000 M4 tanks were produced by the time of V-E Day in May 1945. AUTHOR'S COLLECTION

The M3 37mm antitank cannon was introduced in 1937 as an antiaircraft artillery piece and was the standard weapon in this capacity at the start of the war. At the outbreak of the war in December 1941, this gun was deemed obsolete for an antiaircraft role. However, it was distributed to American infantry units in all theaters as an antitank weapon. In North Africa the 37mm shell could penetrate Vichy French armored cars or the lightly armored Italian tanks; however, it was no match for the German panzers on the battlefield. Weighing just over 900 pounds, the gun could be repositioned by its crew in its immediate vicinity; however, it did need either a jeep or half-track to relocate it to more distant sites. The M3 could fire armor-piercing, high-explosive, and fragmentation ammunition (also called canister). The protective shield for the gun's crew is apparent in this photograph. AUTHOR'S COLLECTION

The versatile M8 75mm pack howitzer was a very suitable infantry support weapon in the mountainous terrain of Tunisia. Its utility was that it could be stripped down into component parts in seconds for animal packs (thus, the term "pack howitzer") or human transport. The M8, with its metal wheels and rubber tires, was introduced in 1936 for mountain and paratroop formations. This relatively light, 1,300-pound howitzer, which fired high-explosive ammunition in support of infantry, was useful at disrupting advancing enemy formations and concentration areas. AUTHOR'S COLLECTION

The 105mm M2A1 howitzer was the U.S. Army's standard field artillery piece for supporting an infantry division. Originally designed in 1928, it did not see extensive production until 1941. The gun's split trail mount can be seen in the photograph. It fired either a high-explosive shell against enemy formations and targets or a hollow charge when used in an antitank role. This howitzer had a maximal range of more than 37,000 feet and was utilized successfully in North Africa, especially at El Guettar in March 1943 against tanks of the 10th Panzer Division. AUTHOR'S COLLECTION

Design and production began late for the 155mm M1 howitzer, and only initial models were available by the war's outbreak; however, by 1945 more than 6,000 had been produced. It was specifically designed to be towed by a motorized vehicle and, although not shown here, had a split trail mount. The gun shield is present for the protection of the crew against counterbattery high-explosive shell bursts. It fired a 95-pound shell a maximum range of 16,000 yards. AUTHOR'S COLLECTION

The 155mm M2 cannon, commonly called a "Long Tom," was one of the most important weapons in the U.S. Army's long-range artillery inventory during World War II and, interestingly, was based on a French design used in World War I. From design to implementation into service took over a decade for the U.S. Army. The Long Tom's carriage, with its ten wheels (eight on its gun mount and two on the trail mount), was specially designed to augment cross-country movement. It had a maximum range of 25,000 yards and fired one 200-pound round per minute. AUTHOR'S COLLECTION

A British Mk II 6-pounder (57mm) antitank gun in a desert camouflage paint scheme. This long-overdue gun, which replaced the obsolete British 2-pounder antitank gun, emerged in its combat debut at the Gazala battle in North Africa in the spring of 1942 and was pivotal at the Alam Halfa and Second Alamein battles in August and October 1942, respectively. Unlike the 2-pounder, which fired only solid shot, the 6-pounder fired high-explosive and armor-piercing rounds, enabling it to be used against Axis batteries and tanks, respectively. Not until the advent of the German Panzer V and Panzer VI would the 6-pounder have trouble defeating these enemy armored vehicles in a direct confrontation, necessitating the deployment of a 17-pounder antitank gun. American factories would also produce an M1 57mm antitank gun based on the 6-pounder design. AUTHOR'S COLLECTION

The bazooka, a rocket-powered recoilless weapon, was introduced into combat during the North African campaign in 1942. During the war almost a half million were manufactured. The bazooka had a range of 300 yards, but for accuracy the target was usually within 100 yards. The weapon had a two-man crew and fired a high-explosive antitank projectile that could also be used against pillboxes, snipers, artillery observers in church steeples, or other enemy positions that were difficult to get close to due to either gunfire or terrain. AUTHOR'S COLLECTION

Four views of the Springfield M1903 bolt-action rifle exhibit the World War I veteran weapon. With the tardy production of the U.S. Army's M1 Garand rifle, the American infantryman entered the war with the M1903. It fired a .30-06-inch caliber bullet with an operational range of under 700 yards. When empty it weighed 8.6 pounds, and it used a five-round magazine. AUTHOR'S COLLECTION

The M1 Garand was the standard-issue rifle of the U.S. Army in World War II as well as the first semiautomatic rifle to enter service with any of the combatant nations' armies. It was gas-operated and entered service in 1936, replacing the Springfield M1903 bolt-action rifle; however, it was not widely distributed to soldiers until 1940. GIs in the assault waves on November 8, 1942, had both the older Springfield M1903 and the new M1 Garand rifles. The M1 Garand fired a .30-06-inch cartridge fed by an eight-round en bloc clip through an internal magazine. A skilled rifleman could fire forty to fifty rounds per minute from this stable gun platform with relatively low recoil, giving this weapon the distinction of the highest sustained rate of fire of any standard-issue rifle during the war. It had an effective range of more than 450 yards; however, its considerable weight of 9.6 pounds (unloaded) was a disadvantage. AUTHOR'S COLLECTION

The Thompson M1928A1 submachine gun was designed during the First World War with the intent of providing infantry squads with a heavy and mobile fire-support weapon to breach enemy trenches—a "trench cleaner"—firing the .45-inch ACP (Automatic Colt Pistol) round. It was heavy, weighing almost 11 pounds empty, and could use box or drum magazines of twenty, thirty, fifty, or one hundred rounds. The Thompson had a maximal operation range of about 220 yards. It was introduced by the U.S. Army in increasing numbers after 1938; however, the production of this firearm was very expensive. AHM, USAHEC, USAWC

The recoil-loading machine pistol, also known as the "grease gun" or "cake decorator," fired the .45-inch (ACP) round and was developed in late 1942 to replace the expensive Thompson submachine gun. The weapon could only fire in full automatic mode and had a detachable magazine of thirty rounds. Primitive in construction compared with the Thompson submachine gun, the M3 was accurate and dirt-resistant but did have some problems with its ammunition feed. It had a cyclic rate of fire of 450 rounds per minute and an effective range of under just 100 yards. AHM, USAHEC, USAWC

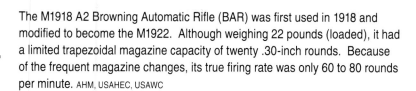

The M1918 A2 Browning Automatic Rifle (BAR) was first used in 1918 and modified to become the M1922. Although weighing 22 pounds (loaded), it had a limited trapezoidal magazine capacity of twenty .30-inch rounds. Because of the frequent magazine changes, its true firing rate was only 60 to 80 rounds per minute. AHM, USAHEC, USAWC

A Remington Rand M1911 A1 semiautomatic pistol which fired a .45-inch ACP bullet from a seven-round magazine. A "robust, reliable and efficient gun" for close quarters combat, it had a range of just over 50 yards. AHM, USAHEC, USAWC

U.S. Army Mk II "pineapple" fragmentation grenade was 3.5 inches in length and packed 2 ounces of explosive charge. It weighed 1.3 pounds, and its serrated configuration maximized the grenade hurler's grip. AUTHOR'S COLLECTION

The Browning M1917 was a heavy machine gun produced in time for service with the American Expeditionary Force in France during World War I. Its service life extended for more than half a century. It was later improved and designated the M1917 A1, and it continued to earn respect as an excellent defensive weapon. Initial models fired a .30-inch caliber round at a cyclic firing rate of 450 rounds per minute, but later designs could reach 600 rounds per minute. It was water-cooled and belt-fed. With a weight of approximately 33 pounds, this machine gun was usually situated in a fixed position and required the bulk of its crew to move it for tactical reasons. Here the venerable M1917 A1 is on a tripod. AUTHOR'S COLLECTION

The Browning M1919 A4 .30-inch caliber medium machine gun provided effective infantry fire support and was light enough for rapid deployment under combat conditions. Adapted from the Browning M1917, this machine gun was air-cooled rather than water-cooled and had a cyclic rate of fire of 400–600 rounds per minute with a range of just over 6,500 feet. It was fed with a 250-round belt of ammunition housed in the attached ammunition box. AUTHOR'S COLLECTION

The Browning M2 .50-inch caliber heavy machine gun on a tripod was used as an infantry support weapon due to its heavy weight. The M2 had tremendous versatility and could be mounted on armored vehicles as well as on aircraft and aboard ships. It had tremendous penetrating power at nonreinforced enemy positions over 2,000 yards away. Used against lightly armored targets, the .50-inch caliber shell could penetrate at over 500 yards. The gun weighed approximately 85 pounds with its tripod and was air-cooled with a perforated jacket. Heavier barrels were incorporated into earlier designs, and these were designated M2HB. AUTHOR'S COLLECTION

The No. 1 Mk III Short Magazine Lee-Enfield (SMLE) bolt action rifle was the primary infantry weapon of British and Commonwealth forces in WWII. It fired a .303-inch cartridge from a ten-round block magazine loaded with five-round charger clips. AUTHOR'S COLLECTION

A British Bren Mk II light machine gun, which was first produced in 1941. It weighed 22.5 pounds and had an overall length of just over 45 inches. Its cyclic rate of fire was only 500 rounds per minute, but it had a range of nearly 3,300 feet. It was gas-operated and air-cooled and fired the standard British .303-inch caliber cartridge in detachable magazines of twenty, thirty, or one hundred rounds, which loaded from the top of the weapon. A Bren crew would typically carry additional replacement barrels. AUTHOR'S COLLECTION

In 1941, production of more than 100,000 inexpensive and simple "Sten" Mk I machine pistols began. Mk II through Mk VI models were also designed with more than 3.5 million ultimately manufactured. The "Sten gun" fired a .35-inch (9mm) round from a thirty-two cartridge magazine. Weighing 6.8 pounds (unloaded), it had an operational range of 200 yards and a firing rate of 500 rounds per minute. AHM, USAHEC, USAWC

The venerable Vickers Mk I medium machine gun fired a .303-inch caliber cartridge and was water-cooled. It weighed 40 pounds and required a team of up to six soldiers to carry and service it. The Vickers was used in World War I, and although it was to be replaced during the interwar years, it remained in service throughout World War II and was not retired until the late 1960s. Its overall length was over 40 inches and its ammunition was belt-fed. Because it had a cyclic rate of fire of 600 rounds per minute and maximum range of just under 10,000 feet, its major use was direct-fire support for infantry. AUTHOR'S COLLECTION

The Webley & Scott service revolver, first designed in 1887, achieved widespread use and renown as the Mk VI with the British Army and Commonwealth troops after its introduction during World War I in 1915. The pistol fired a .455-inch caliber Webley Mk II cartridge from a six-round cylinder, with an effective range of 50 yards, and was rugged enough for the mud and inclement conditions of trench warfare. Many of these guns were still issued to personnel during World War II due to a critical shortage of handguns after hostilities commenced. The pistol had a reputation for excellent stopping power in close quarters. AUTHOR'S COLLECTION

A No. 36 Mills bomb, or hand grenade. This weapon, produced at the Mills factory in Birmingham, England, was introduced to the British Army in 1915 and was the first fragmentation grenade used by Britain. The No. 36 differed from its predecessors in that it had a detachable base to use with a rifle discharger. It was a grooved, cast-iron, pineapple-shaped grenade, with the grooves enhancing the infantryman's grip, and could be thrown about 30 yards; it had a lethal radius of up to 20 yards. World War II–era No. 36 Mills bombs had a shorter-delay fuse of about four seconds, which proved useful against fortified positions. AUTHOR'S COLLECTION

A Parabellum M1908 semiautomatic pistol, commonly referred to as the Luger (named after one of its designers, Georg Luger), utilized a toggle-locking system rather than a slide. The Luger's eight-round detachable box magazine was located in the handgrip, and the weapon fired a .35-inch caliber (9mm) round. The pistol's operational range was approximately 55 yards. Although initially manufactured in 1908 and introduced as the standard handgun of the Kaiser's Imperial Army, it was a favorite of German officers and NCOs in the *Wehrmacht* and *Luftwaffe* during World War II, even though newer and less expensive pistols, such as the Walther semiautomatic handgun, were manufactured in the late 1930s. The Luger was regarded as reliable and accurate but expensive and complicated to manufacture by the Mauser factories in Germany. AUTHOR'S COLLECTION

An MP40 0.35-inch caliber (9mm) Parabellum machine pistol. During the war more than a million MP40 guns (including variants) were manufactured. The weapon had a cyclic rate of fire of 500 rounds per minute in the automatic-fire mode only. The MP40 used a detachable thirty-two-round box magazine, although a sixty-four-round dual-magazine configuration also existed. It was generally considered a reliable weapon, and its folding stock allowed it to be carried with more ease. It was intended for squad or platoon leaders, but on the Russian front it was distributed more widely to match the firepower of similarly sized Soviet units as most of the German infantry were using the standard Mauser 98k standard carbine. AHM, USAHEC, USAWC

A *Panzerschreck*, which means literally "armor fear." This weapon was listed as the *Raketenpanzerbüchse* (RPzB; antitank rocket launcher) 54 and fired a 3.4-inch (88mm) projectile. Its design was based on the U.S. Army bazooka, which was captured during the Tunisian combat and hastily adapted for use by the *Wehrmacht*. Subsequent models would utilize a shield at the front of the barrel to protect the soldier firing the weapon from the gas exhaust of the rocket charge. AHM, USAHEC, USAWC

The general purpose MG 34 German machine gun. It was an air-cooled, belt-fed weapon that fired a 0.3-inch caliber (7.92mm) round. The *Wehrmacht* had been developing a machine gun in 1929 that was lighter than the ones used in World War I but would still have devastating firepower. Although the MG 34 was introduced in 1934, its mass production began two years later, and it proved to be expensive and to require excessive amounts of time for manufacture. It was classified as a light machine gun, weighing just over 25 pounds with its bipod; however, in more fixed positions it could utilize a heavier tripod. It had a cyclic firing rate of 800–900 rounds per minute and could utilize either 50- or 75-round belts or a 300-round drum. Its effective range was over 1,300 yards. The MG 34 was widely used by German infantry during the initial years of the war until the release of the MG 42; however, the former remained as the main machine gun armament for German armored vehicles until the end of the war. AHM, USAHEC, USAWC

A Mauser 98k 0.3-inch caliber (7.92mm) carbine. It was the standard weapon of the German Army's infantry from the mid-1930s and throughout the war. Almost 13 million of these five-round, bolt-action carbines were manufactured as the standard carbine and variants. The design of this shorter carbine emanated from the Kaiser's Imperial Army's standard rifles from 1898 except for the barrel length being reduced. The gun had an operational range of over 400 yards and was equivalent in weight to Allied rifles at approximately 8.5 pounds. AHM, USAHEC, USAWC

An Italian tropical M1928 sun helmet, resplendent with the black plumage of a Bersaglieri infantryman. The helmet gave no protection against bullets or shrapnel. The word *bersaglieri* means "sharpshooter," and since the mid-nineteenth century the Italian Army recruited skilled marksmen and intelligent young men to fill the ranks of these units. There were twelve Bersaglieri regiments employed during World War II. The crest badge on this helmet is indicative of the 5th Regiment. Like the Italian artillery, the Bersaglieri had a reputation for fighting tenaciously during combat. AUTHOR'S COLLECTION

An Italian Mannlicher-Carcano M1891 6.5mm caliber bolt-action, short-barreled carbine. Some of these carbines had folding bayonets, and the Model 91 had an internal six-round box magazine loaded with an en bloc clip. This gun, along with the longer-barrel variant, was the standard rifle for Italian infantrymen in North Africa and had a range of just over 1,600 feet. However, the small caliber and lack of power made the Carcano M1891 largely inferior to the combat rifles of the Allied armies. This carbine was utilized by the Italian Army in World War I, which was emblematic of the lack of weapon modernization of Mussolini's forces in North Africa, since these troops were essentially designed as colonial infantry during the interwar period. Attempts to manufacture a M1938 rifle with a more powerful 7.35mm cartridge were thwarted by supply and production problems, necessitating the continued use of the 6.5mm weapons. AHM, USAHEC, USAWC

An Army chaplain on the left congratulates a GI as he reads a newspaper clipping from home while on the Tunisian front in the spring of 1943. NARA

An American war correspondent wearing a Brodie-style helmet from the interwar years jots down some notes as a U.S. bazooka team moves into Gafsa. At the end of 1942, the M1A1 bazooka was first used by the U.S. Army against the Axis forces in Tunisia. Some of the American bazookas were captured by the Germans, who, based on the U.S. design, developed the *Panzerschreck*. Essentially the bazooka was a metal barrel that was patent at both ends that served as a cylindrical platform to electrically ignite a rocket projectile with a 2.36-inch or 60mm caliber warhead. Now a pair of GIs (loader and discharger) could take on heavily armored targets at a distance. NARA

U.S. Navy chief warrant officer Jack Pennick (left) and an unidentified GI stand next to their M3 half-track upon bivouacking on a cold Tunisian day. In addition to being a U.S. Marine, having served in WWI as well as part of the Peking Legation in China, Pennick joined the U.S. Navy in September 1941 at the age of forty-five and was promoted to the rank of chief warrant officer (chief photographer) in December 1942. Pennick served in the Field Photographic Unit under Comdr. John Ford, the great American film director and Academy Award winner. Pennick was awarded the Silver Star in August 1943 for combat action in North Africa, which explains his presence in this photograph. In addition, Pennick was a film actor, appearing in more than 140 films, many as a costarring member of John Ford's informal stock company. NARA

Soldiers of a Scottish regiment are entertained by one of the pipers in the Egyptian desert at about the time of the Second Battle of El Alamein. It appears that they have seen recent action, as evidenced by some of the soldiers having bandages or blood-stained pullovers. AUTHOR'S COLLECTION

A patrol of Gordon Highlanders of the
51st Highland Division traverse Wadi
Zigzaou during Montgomery's attempt to
outflank the Italians defending the Mareth
Line in southern Tunisia in the spring
of 1943. Natural obstacles such as the
wadis slowed up both infantry and armor
movement. AUTHOR'S COLLECTION

Two members of the Scots Guards inspect a knocked-
out German Panzerkampfwagen (PzKpfw) III near
Medenine in March 1943. This tank has the 75mm gun
with a muzzle counterweight at the end of the barrel.
AUTHOR'S COLLECTION

Leading elements of a British column approaching the
Mareth Line in southern Tunisia. The "Tommies" appear
to be resting when, in fact, they are probably awaiting
sappers to clear more mines to enable their advance.
The white strips serve as indicators of areas to be
avoided because they have not been swept of mines.
NARA

British soldiers of the 50th Division are sleeping in a captured enemy trench after heavy fighting to clear the Italians from those positions on the Mareth Line in southern Tunisia. AWM

Gurkhas in Montgomery's Eighth Army attack over enemy entrenchments with their kukris in hand. AUTHOR'S COLLECTION

Gurkhas of the 4th Indian Division of the Eighth Army show off their kukris (curved knives used in close combat) from a truck to an adoring Tunis crowd flashing the "V for Victory" sign as they enter the former Axis bridgehead on May 10, 1943. NARA

The many different nationalities fighting in North Africa. From left to right, soldiers from Poland, Britain, India, Australia, and Czechoslovakia pose together at Tobruk in October 1941, several months into the state of siege there by Rommel's forces. AWM

Polish infantrymen man a trench on Tobruk's outer perimeter in October 1941. The soldier in the background has his Bren .303-inch caliber light machine gun on an AA stand to be used against low-flying, strafing Axis fighters. AWM

A pair of Greek soldiers man a forward Bren .303-inch caliber light machine gun position in the bleak desert on the Tobruk perimeter in July 1942. The soldier on the right is holding an extra magazine of ammunition for the top-loading gun. AWM

Two Australian soldiers of the 2/13th Infantry Battalion, given the moniker "Desert Rats of Tobruk," smile in December 1941, which marked the lifting of the siege by British forces during Operation Crusader, under Generals Alan Cunningham and Claude Auchinleck. AWM

Indian soldiers in a Punjabi regiment wearing their distinctive turbans. They are guarding Italian prisoners somewhere in the Libyan Desert in December 1941. This photograph was taken by George Silk, who would achieve later fame working as a combat photographer for both the Australian Ministry of Information and, then, *Life* magazine, taking countless action photographs of the Americans and Australians fighting on the northern coast of Papua New Guinea at Buna and Gona. AWM

A Sudanese soldier, as part of the Dominion forces fighting with the British in North Africa, stands guard over Axis prisoners on October 27, 1942, just a few days after the start of Montgomery's Eighth Army offensive at the Second Battle of El Alamein. AWM

Australian gunners, who are now long-term veterans in Montgomery's Eighth Army, stand in front of their 25-pounder field artillery piece as they approach the Mareth Line in southern Tunisia. USAMHI

Maori soldiers from New Zealand eat their meal next to their camouflaged Bren carrier in Tunisia in May 1943. These troops were approaching the Plains of Tunis as the Axis bridgehead there was about to crumble. AWM

After the Center Task Force disembarked soldiers of the U.S. 1st Infantry Division to seize Oran from beaches east and west of the port city, large numbers of Vichy French troops surrendered. Here they are guarded by two American sergeants in the foreground and a few more GIs in the background. NARA

After the Darlan-Clark Armistice was concluded on November 22, 1942, former soldiers for Vichy now became Allied contingents. Unfortunately, they were at a great disadvantage, having obsolete personal weapons and no armor or modern artillery pieces. To be integrated into the Allied Order of Battle, these French soldiers would require refitting, rearming, and retraining. Here a pair of French soldiers, wearing their distinctive Adrian-style helmets, practice firing an American 37mm AT gun, which ironically, too, was obsolete by the standards of combat in Tunisia. USAMHI

French soldiers in combat. Here they are firing a .30-inch caliber machine gun at Axis positions in Tunisia. NARA

French Foreign Legionnaires of Brig. Pierre Koenig's Demi-Brigade sally forth across the open Libyan desert at Bir Hacheim at the southern end of the Gazala Line in the spring of 1942. Ultimately this Free French position fell to Rommel's forces on June 10, 1942, heralding the fall of Tobruk eleven days later. Allied forces would now have to stream back first to Mersa Matruh and then to an incomplete Alamein line, where Auchinleck would halt Rommel's dash for Alexandria, Cairo, and the Suez during chaotic battles in July 1942, which constituted the First Battle of El Alamein. AUTHOR'S COLLECTION

A group of French colonial officers from a Goum unit pose in Bizerte on May 9, 1943, and exhibit the diversity in their uniforms. The officer on the left wears a Spahi gandoura along with a typical French beret. Next to him the second officer wears a woolen djellaba and a white skullcap. The third officer (from left) appears in the more traditional garb of a French Sahara uniform with light-colored kepi. The officer on the far right wears a French police cap and a captured Italian tunic jacket. NARA

A Moroccan Goum sharpens his bayonet for his rifle slung across his back. He wears the classic woolen, striped djellaba of the mountain tribesmen, who were known for their ferocity against Axis soldiers. NARA

Free French colonial troops from Algeria in a mountain artillery unit move up a major road to shell German positions at Pont du Fahs, Tunisia, in 1943. USAMHI

French Senegalese colonial troops clear a path through a minefield, using the more modern metal-detecting minesweeper as well as the older method of probing with a long bayonet, prior to an advance in Tunisia. NARA

Two Italians pose for the camera somewhere in Egypt's Western Desert in mid-1940, after Mussolini cajoled his generals to cross the Egyptian frontier. By their appearance and posture, it seems that this photograph was taken prior to Gen. Sir Richard O'Connor's Operation Compass, which routed the Italians in Egypt and in Cyrenaica from December 1940 to February 1941. This photograph was found by advancing Australian infantry amid the clutter of material left behind by the retreating Italians. AWM

A dead Italian soldier lies behind a stone wall entrenchment at Bardia, which was seized by the Australian 6th Infantry Division in early January 1941. AWM

A dead Italian soldier lies at the bend of an entrenchment at El Alamein in October 1942. Many Italian units, especially the armor and artillery ones, fought bravely. Other units, mostly nonspecialized infantry, were all too happy to surrender or try to escape; however, with limited motor transport, this often was not a viable option, which accounted for the massed Italian surrenders. AWM

An Italian machine gun position behind a stone wall, or sangar, in Tunisia in 1943. The soldier to the left with the binoculars is most likely a Bersaglieri officer, as evidenced by the plumage on his helmet. After the heavy losses in Libya, Italian troops made up the minority of Axis forces in Tunisia. Specialized Italian formations, such as the Bersaglieri, had demonstrated their valor and were considered tough combatants. NARA

A PzKpfw III Ausf. H advances rapidly across the Libyan Desert. This Panzer III model has a 50mm short main turret gun, and due to Hitler's commitment in Russia with his armored forces there, this was one of the most numerous of Rommel's battle tanks in 1942–43. Long-barreled versions of the PzKpfw III and PzKpfw IV would also become more numerous in 1943 and have parity in gun performance with Allied tanks. AUTHOR'S COLLECTION

New Zealanders hold a German tank crew at gunpoint in the Western Desert in 1941. Not an uncommon practice, the Germans captured a Matilda I tank and draped the side of the turret with a Nazi flag and painted a German emblem on the front of the sand skirt. AWM

An American M3 Stuart light tank that was captured by the Nazis has a German emblem painted onto the tank's hull. It was not uncommon for both the Allies and Axis to use captured weaponry to bolster their own forces. This tank was eventually taken back by the Allies at Bizerte. USAMHI

A German prisoner (left) is pressed into service as a litter-bearer to help carry a wounded British Eighth Army soldier near Tunis in the closing days of the campaign in early May 1943. At this time Axis prisoners were surrendering in droves to the Allies. NARA

In Morocco, within hours of the Western Task Force's landings, American troops from the U.S. 7th Infantry Regiment captured German members of the Axis Armistice Commission that was to monitor Vichy French compliance with the stipulations of the agreement from June 1940. The ten Germans abruptly raced out of Fedala in staff cars after the initial landings, only to be captured by American soldiers in the town. The GI at the left carries the older Springfield M1903 rifle with attached bayonet. The newer semiautomatic M1 Garand rifle had not yet been manufactured in sufficient numbers for the majority of combat infantrymen. NARA

In Algiers an Italian Air Force officer with his suitcases leaves his confinement in the Hotel Angleterre under guard for less appealing quarters in a prisoner-of-war stockade outside Algiers. USAMHI

Italian soldiers who surrendered in Tunisia await transport to rear echelon stockades. At least two Italian prisoners in this group have either a suitcase or knapsack packed. USAMHI

German prisoners of war are assigned to U.S. Army two-man tents behind the barbed-wire enclosure of a stockade outside Tunis. The prisoners had recently received delousing showers after having been in their fieldworks for an extended period. NARA

An Italian soldier lies dead near a fishing boat at Tabeul, Cape Bon. Rather than surrendering, many Axis soldiers attempted to take refuge there in what Allied commanders feared would become a final redoubt after Tunis and Bizerte were captured. Also, some of the Axis forces sought out small boats to try to escape to Sicily from Cape Bon, which is at the very north end of the peninsula that has the Gulf of Tunis and the Mediterranean Sea as water boundaries. NARA

A dead *Wehrmacht* soldier lies sprawled amid shell casings of the 88mm AA/AT dual-purpose gun that he was manning near Tunis in early May 1943. AUTHOR'S COLLECTION

A dead German soldier lies next to an automobile at Sened Station, which the U.S. II Corps attacked on March 20–23, 1943, in the central Tunisia sector. At this juncture the Americans had begun their recovery from the twin, devastating defeats at Sidi Bou Zid and Kasserine Pass, on February 14 and February 20, respectively, and would continue the counteroffensive east. USAMHI

CHAPTER 4

THE AMPHIBIOUS LANDINGS

WESTERN TASK FORCE

The Western Task Force's assault on Safi by Maj. Gen. Ernest Harmon's forces would be confronted by French batteries as well as a garrison of fewer than 1,000 men. There would not be any preparatory naval bombardment, as it was Eisenhower's desire that if there were to be opposition from the Vichy French forces, they would have to fire first. As the naval force turned toward the assault beaches, the French commenced firing and the U.S. Navy immediately returned fire targeting the French batteries. In the early-morning hours, elements of the U.S. 47th Infantry Regiment landed, and by sunrise the port was captured with only sporadic sniper fire. Well before noon all Vichy batteries had been neutralized by U.S. naval gunfire.

Both high surf and darkness caused landing accidents that delayed the off-loading of vehicles and artillery. Despite not all of the assault troops disembarking from their transports by noon due to heavy seas, the local Vichy commander at Safi surrendered by midafternoon, although resistance continued from other localities. Keeping the French around Safi in their positions, Harmon began his armored trek north to surround Casablanca, which had more than 4,000 troops, from the rear.

At Port Lyautey, 220 miles up the Moroccan coast, French opposition was much stronger than at Safi, with aircraft capable of strafing the landing beaches as well as bomb transports. Also, there was a strong coast artillery concentration at the Mehdia fortress, which was to fire a heavy volume of shells at the transports offshore, and in turn this site was bombarded. The fortress's garrison surrendered after Navy Scout Bomber Douglas (SBD) Dauntless dive-bombers made an initial attack. There were also Vichy French reinforcements from Rabat that would add to the fire on American assault troops. As at Safi, heavy seas slowed debarkation during the early-morning darkness of November 8 and contributed to many of the assault battalions landing miles away from their assigned beaches. By nightfall Truscott's troops were still miles from the Port Lyautey airfield that was surrounded by the Sebou River. D-Day plus one provided some American gains against the Vichy

defenders; however, the airfield was not surrounded until November 10 with the assistance of the U.S. Navy destroyer-transport *Dallas*, which ran a gauntlet of enemy artillery fire as it steamed up the Sebou River with assault troops. At 4 A.M. on November 11, a ceasefire commenced, with Truscott having controlled his objectives.

At Fedala, 70 miles to the south of Mehdia, the Vichy French garrison forces numbered 2,500 troops, with some coastal batteries possessing large-caliber artillery pieces. Individual battalion landing teams came ashore at four sites along 4 miles of coastline with the intent to seize Fedala as well as control all roads and rail lines leading to it from Casablanca, only 12 miles to the south. Rough seas and a strong current caused chaos in the landings at Fedala, scattering and drowning assault troops as well as destroying landing craft and vehicles. More than 50 percent of the initial assault wave's landing craft were put out of commission, which delayed subsequent infantry, equipment, and supply reinforcement. The plan to rapidly seize Casablanca from the immediate north of the port city had devolved. Nonetheless, tactical improvisation by the scattered American assault forces that came ashore at 5 A.M. on November 8 enabled Fedala's capture within hours; however, French battery fire, especially at the mouth of the Nefifikh River and at Cap de Fedala, would require several more hours of American infantry assault to silence them. With that occurrence Patton's transports could anchor closer to the beach and use Fedala's port facilities to hasten the chaotic and tardy off-loading of reinforcements, armor, and supplies.

From Casablanca a French cruiser, accompanied by destroyers and submarines, sortied out of the port and, together with the guns of the battleship *Jean Bart* and Vichy aircraft, initiated fire on the Western Task Force's flagship, *Augusta*, with Rear Adm. H. Kent Hewitt and Maj. Gen. George S. Patton aboard. Almost five hours of a naval surface action, combined with a vigorous U.S. Navy carrier-borne aircraft defense, were required to compel the French warships to retreat.

On D-Day plus one Maj. Gen. Jonathan Anderson moved four battalions of infantry south along the coast for his assault on Casablanca, with its population of more than 200,000 residents, which was scheduled for D-Day plus two; however, due to unloading problems he had only a fraction of his vehicles and supplies as well as a lack of land-based air support. These factors caused him to halt his southward march 6 miles north of Casablanca. The majority of Anderson's armor was still aboard the transports offshore of Fedala.

At midnight on November 9–10, Anderson resumed his march toward Casablanca; however, French artillery fire and infantry assaults along with French naval gunfire from the port delayed the Brushwood force, halting it on the eastern and southern outskirts of the city. By 5 P.M. on November 10, the Americans had suffered about 150 casualties, with more than 30 killed in action that day. Patton's chief of staff, Col. Hobart R. Gay, was sent to negotiate an armistice with Vichy French general Charles-Auguste-Paul Noguès, aptly on November 11, after the French had sent out a ceasefire order at 7 P.M. on November 10.

CENTER TASK FORCE

The defenses at Oran were formidable, including 13 coastal batteries, 17,000 Vichy French troops, as well as 100 aircraft and several French Navy destroyers in the harbor. There were also more than a dozen French seaplanes at Oran. Maj. Gen. Lloyd R. Fredendall's Center Task Force was to commence its amphibious landings at 1 A.M. on November 8; however, similar problems were encountered, such as a strong ocean current and confusion about the proper location of several cargo ships. Nonetheless, the assault troops reached land, albeit late and sometimes at the incorrect destination. Surprisingly, there was no artillery fire from French batteries. The village of Lourmel, southwest of Oran, was quickly seized by an American armored column. Brig. Gen. Theodore "Ted" Roosevelt, the assistant commander of the 1st Infantry Division who was also leading the 26th Regimental Combat Team's (RCT) assault on Beach Y, between Lourmel and Oran, overcame some initial operational difficulties by 6:45 A.M. and then proceeded to destroy some French armored cars and capture two Algerian villages by midmorning. His advance occurred simultaneously with the sinking of a French warship along with British naval suppressive gunfire on French batteries shelling the transports. However, Vichy gunfire from elevated terrain brought his 26th RCT to a halt.

Maj. Gen. Terry Allen's 16th and 18th RCTs from his 1st Infantry Division, with accompanying armor of Combat Command B of the 1st Armored Division and the attached 1st Ranger Battalion under Maj. William O. Darby, respectively, assaulted Beach Z, 20 miles to the east of Oran between Arzew and St. Leu, without opposition and moved inland. The attached Rangers captured two coastal batteries after assaulting them from the rear. However, the easy advances ceased at the village of St. Cloud when the 18th RCT met intense Vichy fire.

The 16th RCT made excellent progress in seizing villages and defeating a colonial unit before embarking inland to the southwest to attack and seize Tafaraoui airfield, 25 miles away. The Vichy French had a large number of fighter-bombers there (as well as at La Sénia), which posed a threat to the transports offshore. The French Dewoitine planes, which were more maneuverable than the Allied carrier-borne fighters, were piloted by experienced Vichy airmen. The airfield's seizure was accomplished during the afternoon, and Maj. Gen. James Doolittle's Twelfth Air Force British Spitfire squadrons, previously stationed on Gibraltar, fought off French planes and landed at Tafaraoui, giving the Allies their first land-based air facility. On D-Day plus one Vichy French resistance stiffened, with attacks on both the 16th and 26th RCTs at Beaches Z and Y, respectively, which failed. A French armored column was also turned back in its movement on the now occupied Allied airfield at Tafaraoui. Also, the airfield at La Sénia was quickly occupied by American ground forces after French pilots flew most of their planes to other locations.

Allen kept a holding action at St. Cloud, where the French resistance was still tenacious, and took an armored column around the position on November 9. At dawn on the following day, Allen's armored force moved into Oran from the south, seizing the commander's headquarters and the port. By the end of D-Day plus one, Oran would be hemmed in on all sides by 1st Infantry Division forces and the two main airfields south of the port city, Tafaraoui and La Sénia, would be in Allied hands. At noon on D-Day plus two, a ceasefire was initiated, with a surrender of French forces a few hours later.

Operation Reservist, which had the lofty objective of compelling Oran's surrender with a coup de main entrance of Oran harbor with American infantrymen aboard two British cutters, turned into a fiasco after receiving withering fire from French shore battery and destroyer gunfire. Of the 400 soldiers aboard, only 47 Americans landed, while both Royal Navy vessels burned and eventually sank.

EASTERN TASK FORCE

Maj. Gen. Charles Ryder's amphibious forces were to land along three beaches that stretched along roughly 50 miles of coast. Beaches Apples and Beer, to the west of Algiers, were to be assaulted by the British 11th Infantry Brigade Group and 168th RCT of the U.S. 34th Infantry Division, respectively. To the east of Algiers, along Beach Charlie, the 39th RCT from the 9th U.S. Infantry Division would land and seize the villages of Surcouf and Ain Taya while neutralizing French shore batteries in Cap Matifou. In this manner Algiers would be invested from the west, south, and east. Fortunately, there was no Vichy French opposition at Beaches Apples and Beer. The British amphibious assault at Beach Apples was the easiest of all the Torch landings. The airfield at Blida, 12 miles inland, was seized early on D-Day. However, at Beach Beer, the ubiquitous problems of the high surf and the novelty of large-scale amphibious operations left the 168th RCT and elements of British Commandos strewn across many miles of beach.

The French did mount a response to the landings at Beach Charlie, with shore battery gunfire adding to the problem of high surf. Nonetheless, the 39th RCT troops moved over 8 miles inland, taking the Maison Blanche airfield by 8:30 A.M. An Allied transport and destroyer were damaged by Axis aircraft, while intermittent French shore gunfire was silenced. For Algiers an operation similar to the one in Oran harbor, Operation Terminal, involved a battalion of the U.S. 135th Infantry Regiment aboard two Royal Navy destroyers. However, this forced assault on a defended port ended in failure as well.

As sporadic combat engagements continued around Algiers on D-Day, negotiations for a ceasefire were under way with Adm. Francois Darlan, who was authorized by the Vichy France leader, the elderly Marshal Pétain, to act as he deemed appropriate for the combat conditions. Darlan concluded a ceasefire for 8 P.M. on November 8, but only for his Algiers forces. As mentioned previously, it was not until 12:15 P.M. and 7:10 P.M. on November 10 that ceasefires were instituted in Oran and Casablanca, respectively. In all, fewer than 1,500 Allied casualties were incurred during the initial landings of Operation Torch, with the overwhelming majority being American since more than two-thirds of the Allied force was from U.S. units. Fortunately for the Allies, only token French infantry resistance was encountered and shore battery fire was addressed with surface ship bombardment and carrier-borne air sorties.

Adolf Hitler's reaction to the Torch landings was easy to comprehend. Unoccupied France was seized, and the Vichy government was ended. A race to Tunis now ensued as the situation in the French colony of Tunisia was now fluid. Unfortunately, the Nazi leader occupied the Tunisian bridgehead with a new German contingent, since Rommel was about to retreat from El Alamein. A 5th Panzer Army, arriving in the Tunisian ports of Tunis and Bizerte by aircraft and ships from Italy, would achieve the quickest buildup of forces, thereby deterring Lt. Gen. Kenneth A.N. Anderson's British First Army marching east from Algeria to capture the French colony. By mid-December the Tunisian frontier was locked in a stalemate, as the Allies were too weak to defeat the Axis defenses and the 5th Panzer Army was still too poorly supplied for a major offensive thrust to push Anderson's army back into Algeria. Campaigning in the Tunisian winter was put on hold by the Allies, and plans were drawn up for a major spring offensive. However, the Germans would have other plans.

The deck of an Allied troopship is packed with U.S. soldiers as it moves in convoy toward one of three landing zones for Operation Torch. The Western Task Force convoy, under Patton, sailed from the United States. The Center and Eastern Task Forces, with a total of thirty-nine transports and escorting warships, would depart southward from the Firth of Clyde near Glasgow. NARA

American soldiers on the deck of an Allied transport as it sails for North Africa. As fears of prowling Nazi U-boats were always extant, the soldiers are wearing life jackets. Also, life rafts hang suspended from the side of the ship, along with antiaircraft (AA)/antishipping naval guns at the right and in the background. NARA

An aerial view from a U.S. airplane of the convoy as it sails in column with destroyers in the lead and on the flanks to one of three destinations: Northwest Africa's Atlantic coast near Casablanca in French Morocco (Western Task Force); Oran in Algeria (Center Task Force); and farther to the east in Algeria, the port of Algiers (Eastern Task Force). NARA

American soldiers test-fire their rifles from the deck of the transport *Monarch of Bermuda* two days before the North African invasion on November 6, 1942. In the background is another of the convoy's vessels steaming in column with the troopship. NARA

A U.S. Navy Grumman F4F Wildcat fighter prepares to take off from the deck of the American carrier USS *Ranger* to support the Moroccan landings at Fedala on November 8, 1942. It was from the port city of Casablanca, with its strong Vichy French naval presence and accompanying airfields, that the Allies feared strong resistance to the amphibious landings. In fact, the French battleship *Jean Bart* was stationary and moored in Casablanca harbor; however, it fired its 15-inch guns at the Western Task Force, drawing American counterfire, which destroyed the Vichy vessel. Under cover of a Vichy naval smokescreen, French destroyers and cruisers sortied from the port. Despite the presence of the *Ranger*'s Wildcats aloft, French naval shelling of the American destroyers USS *Ludlow* and USS *Wilkes* scored two hits on the former and compelled the

latter to pull back to sea. Several of the French destroyers were sunk, and other vessels were forced to retreat back into Casablanca after being damaged by successful bombing sorties by the Wildcats from the *Ranger*. An American tanker converted into an escort aircraft carrier, the USS *Santee*, along with the British aircraft carrier HMS *Argus*, operated off Safi in Morocco and Algiers with the Western and Eastern Task Forces, respectively, during the invasion, with sorties of aircraft to suppress both French ground movements at the former landing zone and, for the latter site, an air response from the airfield at Blida in Algeria. HMS *Furious*, with two auxiliary carriers, was 30 miles offshore of Oran supporting the Center Task Force with Seafires (the Royal Navy's Spitfire equivalent) and Hurricanes. NARA

American soldiers of the U.S. 1st Infantry Division aboard a troop transport of the Center Task Force bound for landing beaches near Oran enjoy a lighter moment in the anxious times on November 8, 1942, before climbing into landing craft. Note that the GIs have an American flag sewn onto their left shoulder (far right) to garner some favor with the Vichy French troops that they anticipated meeting. USAMHI

American soldiers of a heavy weapons platoon with the Center Task Force load their gear onto a wooden pallet that they will then lower with the ropes that they are attaching. USAMHI

Men of the 1st Ranger Battalion rehearse getting off of the transport's sides and into landing craft for the run-in to Arzew, northeast of Oran, which was one of the targets of the Center Task Force. The Rangers were to be tasked with neutralizing some French gun forts on the coast, which if not captured would enfilade the D-Day landings of the 18th Regimental Combat Team (RCT) of the U.S. 1st Infantry Division. NARA

Off the coast of Oran, an M3 half-track sits within the well of a landing craft while a 37mm antitank (AT) gun is lowered over the side of the transport. This latter weapon, soon to be obsolete, would be effective against French armored cars and fortified pillboxes; however, it would be no match for the German Panzer III and IV tanks of the *Wehrmacht* soon after the landings. USAMHI

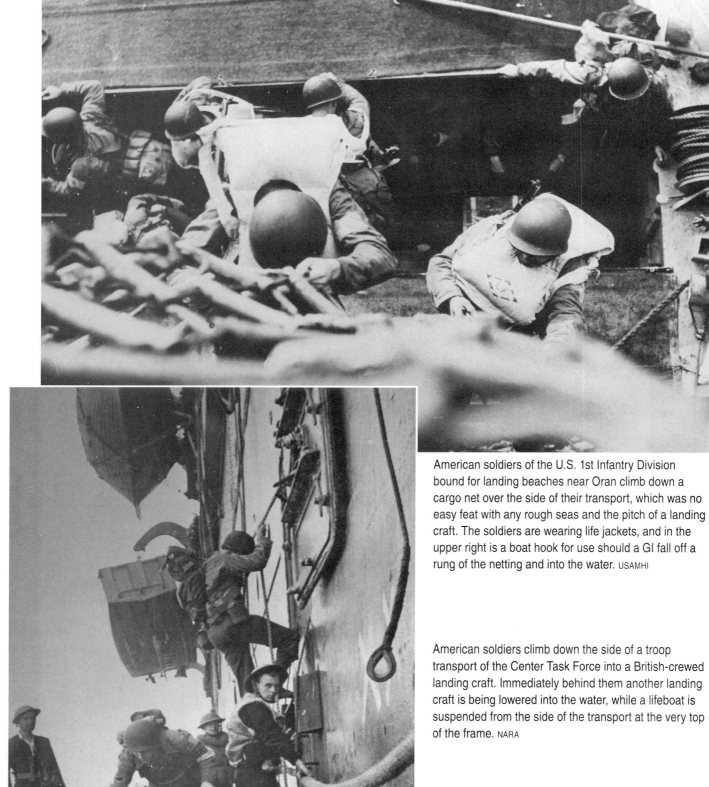

American soldiers of the U.S. 1st Infantry Division bound for landing beaches near Oran climb down a cargo net over the side of their transport, which was no easy feat with any rough seas and the pitch of a landing craft. The soldiers are wearing life jackets, and in the upper right is a boat hook for use should a GI fall off a rung of the netting and into the water. USAMHI

American soldiers climb down the side of a troop transport of the Center Task Force into a British-crewed landing craft. Immediately behind them another landing craft is being lowered into the water, while a lifeboat is suspended from the side of the transport at the very top of the frame. NARA

Soldiers of the U.S. 1st Infantry Division's 16th RCT huddle down within their British-crewed landing craft as it makes its run-in to the Algerian beach near St. Leu, to the northeast of Oran, on November 8, 1942. Another landing craft follows them, with the troopship in the background. NARA

Three American sergeants, each of a different rank, sit anxiously within their landing craft during their run-in to one of the several Allied beachheads on November 8, 1942. A multitude of landing beaches were chosen, since attacks on defended ports were deemed risky after the disaster at Dieppe in August 1942 and would again be proven tactically incorrect as British destroyers laden with U.S. infantry would suffer grievously. NARA

An American soldier has yet to board a U.S. Navy patrol–aircraft rescue boat for a trip into Safi on Morocco's Atlantic coast. Safi is located far to the south of both Casablanca and its nearby landing beach zone at Fedala. Maj. Gen. Ernest Harmon was commanding the American assault of Sub–Task Force Blackstone there. It was defended by a French Army barracks with only 450 men of the 2nd Moroccan Infantry Regiment, but the local Vichy commander had several batteries of fixed coastal guns and mobile guns as well as the use of an emergency Vichy airfield. NARA

Several landing craft mechanized (LCMs) circle a transport to group as an assault wave for the run-in to the Safi landing zone on Morocco's Atlantic coast south of Casablanca. General Harmon, commander of Sub–Task Force Blackstone, had worried for months that high surf would hamper his landings on D-Day; however, the sea off Safi was calm. Safi was an ancient Moroccan town with a population of 25,000. NARA

An American heavy weapons squadron in a British-crewed landing craft makes its final approach to a landing beach near Oran on D-Day. The troops' leader is giving some final instructions before the ramp will be lowered. The fighting in and around Oran was fierce as there was a strong Vichy French response to the landings by both local garrison troops as well as coastal batteries that needed to be seized. USAMHI

British landing craft taking American troops to beach zones near Fedala on Morocco's Atlantic coast, just miles to the northeast of Casablanca, encounter some rough surf, which drenches them with ocean spray, during the run-in. Elements of the U.S. 3rd Infantry Division assigned to the Sub–Task Force Brushwood, commanded by Maj. Gen. Jonathan Anderson, made the assault at Fedala. The rough surf swept many landing craft into disarray, with some crashing into rocks or capsizing, resulting in GIs drowning with their heavy kit and weaponry. NARA

Rough surf off the coast of Fedala is evident as landing craft crewman try to steer their shallow-draft wooden vessels toward the landing beaches. Unfortunately, many craft hit razor-sharp reefs instead of designated beaches, resulting not only in injuries but in GIs reaching shore without their weapons and equipment. NARA

Near Safi, Gen. Ernest Harmon's second wave of landing craft, which were to reinforce previous elements of the U.S. 3rd Infantry Division, arrive at the beach. In this aerial view infantrymen scampering from their landing craft are evident at the shoreline, as are the tracks in the sand of previous wheeled vehicles heading inland. NARA

An LCM destroyed at Fedala due to the high surf there. As dawn approached, it became apparent that more than 60 of the 116 assault craft that embarked from the American transports offshore were now wrecked. Nonetheless, elements of the U.S. 7th Infantry Regiment rallied and organized themselves once ashore and rushed into Fedala. NARA

The Mehdia Kasbah, a centuries-old, thick-walled Spanish fortress that guarded the Sebou River and ground approaches to Port Lyautey, was heavily shelled as part of the U.S. 60th Infantry Regiment of the 3rd Division's assault. Port Lyautey was the second-most-important anchorage in French Morocco, 6 miles inland from the Mehdia Beach and only a few miles from a French air complex with concrete runways and modern hangars. Despite the bombardment, Vichy French fortifications, often perched atop hills, held out for a few days against American assault by air, sea, and ground. The final assault by U.S. ground troops as part of Sub–Task Force Goalpost, under Brig. Lucian Truscott, incurred more than 225 casualties to seize the bastion guarding the Sebou River and the approach to the airdrome. Truscott's assault was supported by the USS *Chenango*, an oiler that was converted in early 1942 into an escort carrier, with a complement of more than 70 P-40 Warhawks that eventually landed at the captured airfield. Other Allied planes of the Twelfth Air Force were to be flown in from Gibraltar. NARA

The Mehdia Beach, a prewar resort, with a view of a coastal fort that was captured early on November 8, 1942, as a prelude to the assault on Port Lyautey, which was 6 miles inland on the Sebou River and guarded by the Mehdia Kasbah citadel atop a hill. NARA

American soldiers of Major General Harmon's Sub–Task Force Blackstone come ashore from the surf with an AA gun being towed out of the surf to bolster the Allied beachhead near Safi. In the background Allied transports lie very close to the shore. The surf at Safi was uncharacteristically calm on D-Day. NARA

American soldiers walk down the stair ramps of a landing craft infantry (LCI) onto the beach at Safi in French Morocco as part of Sub–Task Force Blackstone's reinforcement waves. D-Day, November 8, 1942, was one of only roughly a dozen days when a calm sea could be expected along the Atlantic coast of French Morocco, and General Harmon's forces were quite fortunate as placid surf conditions greeted the initial and subsequent amphibious landings. NARA

Two American soldiers guard wrecked LCMs that struck rocks and reefs due to the high surf at Fedala, to the northwest of Casablanca. Both soldiers pose with their M1928 Thompson .45-inch caliber submachine guns. NARA

An American flag flies over a Vichy French–occupied coastal fort at Pointe de la Tour to the north of the town of Safi, which was assaulted by Major General Harmon's Sub–Task Force Blackstone. When a platoon of assault troops from the U.S. 47th Infantry Division arrived, they found the French 130mm guns silenced, with their gunners dead, as a result of the naval bombardment by the venerable American battleship USS *New York*. NARA

An aerial view of the harbor at Safi, far to the south of Casablanca, after its capture by Major General Harmon's Sub–Task Force Blackstone. A U.S. Navy Scout Bomber Douglas (SBD) Dauntless dive bomber flies overhead to the right, with Allied ships offshore in the background. NARA

At Oran a British destroyer in the Center Task Force lays
a smokescreen while empty British-crewed landing craft
(foreground) return to their transports. AUTHOR'S COLLECTION

An American soldier carries an unfurled Stars and Stripes as
he crosses a narrow-gauge railway track close to the shoreline
at Oran. It was hoped that the display of American flags, either
carried or worn as shoulder patches by the infantrymen, would
discourage the Vichy French forces from firing. However, despite
the national identification, American forces were engaged in sharp
firefights with the French defenders at the several assault beaches
attacked in and around Oran on D-Day. NARA

A British landing craft attached to the Center Task Force disembarks American troops and equipment of the U.S. 1st Infantry Division at a beach in Oran as part of a subsequent, reinforcing amphibious wave on D-Day. AUTHOR'S COLLECTION

American troops of the U.S. 18th RCT of the 1st Infantry Division wade ashore from a British landing craft onto a landing beach near Arzew on D-Day. Allied transports lie close to shore in the right and background, while a destroyer can be faintly seen in the left background. USAMHI

As seen from an Allied landing craft, recently disembarked GIs wade ashore without incident toward an Algerian beach near Oran. To the west and east of Oran, there were seven beaches where Allied troops landed. They were designated as areas X, Y, and Z, with White and Green beaches for each area and an additional Red beach for area Z. Armored forces of the 1st Armored Division came ashore at the two most remote points from Oran. X White and Green beaches to the west of Oran at Mersa Bou Zedjar were assigned to Col. Paul Robinett's Task Force Green of the 1st Armored Division. Z Red beach, the farthest east from the port city, was near St. Leu. The U.S. 1st Infantry Division's 26th RCT came ashore at Y White and Green beaches in the vicinity of Les Andalouses. The 1st Ranger Battalion and elements of the 18th RCT of the 1st Infantry Division landed at Z Green beach at Arzew. The 16th RCT of the 1st Infantry Division disembarked from their landing craft at Z White and Red beaches near St. Leu. NARA

At Arzew elements of the 1st Infantry Division come ashore as a subsequent wave bringing equipment and ammunition on D-Day. Note the proximity of the transports and scattered landing craft to the shoreline. USAMHI

As one Ranger remains poised with his .30-inch caliber Browning machine gun pointed in the direction of resisting Vichy French troops, other Rangers from the 1st Ranger Battalion relax after the capture of a French coastal gun emplacement at Arzew on November 8, 1942. Allied intelligence had reported that the sea approaches between Oran and Arzew had thirteen such batteries of large-caliber coastal guns that also had the capability of being turned inward. NARA

Rangers from the 1st Battalion kick open a door to a building in Arzew in which they suspect Vichy French soldiers are hiding. The invasion planners knew before D-Day that the Center Task Force might fight with Vichy's Oran Division of 10,000 men. An additional 12,500 Vichy French troops could also be summoned and arrive at the battlefield within five days. NARA

Two corporals from the 1st
Ranger Battalion cover a French
gun battery above Arzew harbor
to the east of Oran on D-Day.
The Ranger in the foreground
is armed with the relatively new
M1 semiautomatic Garand rifle,
while the one behind him is
aiming his Springfield M1903
bolt-action rifle, which, although
very accurate, firing a heavy-
caliber round, could not match
the Garand in rate of fire. NARA

American soldiers of the 26th RCT, 1st Infantry Division, under Brig. Gen. Theodore Roosevelt Jr., man a .50-inch caliber heavy AA
machine gun at Les Andalouses, to the west of Oran in Algeria. Other soldiers are dug in with some camouflage over their foxholes in
anticipation of Axis air strikes. NARA

American riflemen of the 26th RCT of the U.S. 1st Infantry Division man their M1 Garand weapons in foxholes along an Algerian road at Les Andalouses. The landing there was uncontested during the early-morning hours of November 8, 1942. GIs found Vichy French soldiers asleep in houses near the shoreline of this former Algerian beach resort. NARA

A Vichy French White-Laffy armored car of the *Chasseurs d'Afrique* (Huntsmen of Africa cavalry corps) sits disabled after coming under fire from an American 37mm AT gun of the 26th RCT on D-Day at El Ancor, inland from Les Andalouses landing beach, west of Oran. The Djebel Murdjadjo ridge, which runs west to east from Les Andalouses to the western outskirts of Oran, is in the background. NARA

Allied troops inspect some of the damage inflicted on Oran's buildings after the combat for the Algerian port city ended. An M3 half-track stands in the left background. Prior to the American arrival at Oran, there was also extensive fighting leading into Oran from the east on D-Day plus one. At St. Cloud, a village of 4,000 Algerians, French colonial infantry contested an advance of the 1st Ranger Battalion and elements of the 18th RCT of the 1st Infantry Division moving in from Arzew. After overcoming some fortified positions, Gen. Terry de la Mesa Allen, the commanding general of the U.S. 1st Infantry Division, chose to bypass and isolate the remainder of St. Cloud. NARA

An American two-and-a-half-ton truck hauling a 37mm AT gun from a British landing barge attempts to negotiate the soft sand at Les Andalouses, west of Oran. Brigadier Roosevelt's 26th RCT of the 1st Infantry Division had landed there earlier in the dark early-morning hours of D-Day. USAMHI

British soldiers watch as an American-manned two-and-a-half-ton truck pulling an artillery piece leaves a British landing craft at Les Andalouses, west of Oran, on D-Day plus one. Another British LCM to transport vehicles and artillery sits on the shoreline in the background. NARA

An American bulldozer is employed on D-Day plus one to off-load vehicles from reinforcing waves of British landing craft to hasten the buildup of supplies and vehicles for the continued drive on Oran. The soft sand at Les Andalouses, west of Oran, had slowed down the disembarkation of vehicles from landing craft. NARA

An American M3 half-track hauling a 37mm AT gun behind it has a bit of tough going through the soft sand on the beach at Les Andalouses, west of Oran, on D-Day. Les Andalouses, which was a beach resort for Europe's wealthy before the war, was deserted of Vichy opposition for the landings of the 26th RCT of the 1st Infantry Division. USAMHI

At Surcouf, at the very eastern end of the Allied landing by the Eastern Task Force to seize Algiers, American and British troops work hard to push an American jeep out of the soft sand of that Algerian beach on D-Day. USAMHI

At Les Andalouses beach, to the west of Oran, Army engineers try to combat the soft sand that had been delaying the off-loading of Allied vehicles and artillery on D-Day by laying roadbed steel wire framework over burlap. The houses in the background comprise what was once a beach resort for wealthy Europeans before the war. NARA

Unloading of men and equipment at St. Leu, which was the easternmost beach assaulted by the 16th RCT of the 1st Infantry Division and elements of the 1st Armored Division, all of the Center Task Force, on D-Day. Army engineers are busy laying down steel matting in the right foreground, which was to facilitate off-loading of vehicles and artillery from the landing craft. Numerous transports and landing craft are close to the shoreline after the initial successful amphibious assault. USAMHI

A medical team with litter-bearers of the U.S. 1st Infantry Division is brought ashore by a British LCM, seen offshore in the background, in a subsequent landing wave on D-Day plus two. An American bulldozer is trying to smooth the sand after previous heavy vehicular and artillery traffic. USAMHI

American soldiers of the 1st Infantry Division march in formation down a well-preserved cobblestoned street in Oran on D-Day plus four, as the Center Task Force tries to accelerate the buildup of Allied troops after the successful landings. Hitler, who initially praised the Vichy French ground, air, and naval forces combating the Allied invasion at both Oran and Casablanca, denounced them after a ceasefire had been agreed upon following heavy fighting to seize both the Western and Center Task Forces' port objectives. On D-Day plus one the *Wehrmacht* had begun pouring troops and *Luftwaffe* aircraft into Tunisia. Some French forces, under Gen. George Barré, the Vichy ground forces commander in Tunisia, in a move to stay out of Nazi control, began to withdraw west to Algeria. NARA

American soldiers climb down cargo nets (background) and a ladder suspended from a hull hatch door of a troop transport of the Eastern Task Force (foreground) into waiting British-crewed landing craft for the run-in toward landing beaches around Algiers, 270 miles east of Oran. The city of Algiers was spread out over a 16-mile-long bay and had a civilian population of 300,000, and the landing beaches were well to the east and west of the port. After reaching shore, the Allied landing forces were instructed to move inland quickly to seize the airfields at Blida and Maison Blanche, respectively. USAMHI

American troops disembark from British-crewed landing craft later in the day on D-Day; a transport and another approaching landing craft are in the background. The 168th Infantry Regiment of the U.S. 34th Division was to land at White and Green beaches in the Beer sector but was scattered in the darkness early on D-Day along 15 miles of Algerian coastline. The U.S. 39th Infantry Regiment of the 9th Division was to land at the most eastern point of the amphibious assault, at Surcouf. AUTHOR'S COLLECTION

British assault troops of the more than 7,000-strong 11th Infantry Brigade land unopposed as they disembark from an LCM at the Apples sector's Green beach, 20 miles southwest of Algiers near the small coastal town of Castiglione. A small building is in the right background. At other beaches to the west of Algiers, French troops surrendered without firing on the British infantry. AUTHOR'S COLLECTION

British troops haul a wheeled cart through some soft sand at one of their landing beaches in the Apples sector while other infantrymen get a motorcycle operational in the right background. At some locales, such as Fort Duperré, just on the outskirts of the western side of Algiers, the local Vichy French commander decided to ignore French general Charles-Emmanuel Mast's order to cooperate with the Allies and instead obey French general Louis-Marie Koeltz's instructions to resist the invasion. Koeltz was later to serve the Allied cause well as commander of the French 19th Corps in Tunisia, drawing praise from Eisenhower in his fighting of the Axis forces there. AUTHOR'S COLLECTION

A road sign for Surcouf, 20 miles east of Algiers, which was the site of the Eastern Task Force's eastern flank of amphibious landings. The landing zones for this assault were in the Charlie area at beaches 1 and 2, with Surcouf being in the middle of the two designated beaches. The 39th RCT of the U.S. 9th Infantry Division made the assault. USAMHI

American troops of the 39th RCT of the U.S. 9th Infantry Division quickly run up the beach after disembarking from their landing craft at Surcouf on November 8, 1942. An American flag is unfurled as the leading troops approach a rise in the sand to the left. It was anticipated that the showing of American flags unfurled and on the shoulders of U.S. troops would deter the local French forces from firing on them; however, this ploy failed. Nonetheless, a ceasefire was declared by the French military leaders in Algiers during the midafternoon of D-Day. Interestingly, the American landing force contingent in the Eastern Task Force was much smaller than its British counterpart. NARA

American equipment being landed at Algiers after D-Day and the ensuing ceasefire. In the midafternoon on D-Day, in the midst of heavy gunfire and more than twelve hours after the initial Allied landings, the Vichy French commanders, Adm. Francois Darlan and Gen. Alphonse Juin, decided to surrender Algiers. The pair contacted the American envoy, Robert Murphy, who in turn went to Gen. Charles Ryder to inform him of Darlan's order for all French forces in the Algiers area to obey a ceasefire. AUTHOR'S COLLECTION

An American officer with some of his soldiers questions a French officer in Algiers after a ceasefire had been declared by Admiral Darlan. More-formal conversations between Lt. Gen. Mark Clark, the Allied deputy commander, and an array of French admirals and generals started in Algiers on the morning of November 10, 1942. Although a ceasefire was in effect, the local French commanders had been reluctant to bring their forces into the Allied camp without formal authorization from Marshal Pétain in Vichy. AUTHOR'S COLLECTION

After a ceasefire had been declared following several hours of fighting on D-Day, American soldiers with their equipment and bedrolls march along the quay of Algiers harbor after disembarking from the troopship in the background. Another ship prepares to enter the harbor behind the docked one. NARA

An American main regimental signals radio station is partially secluded in a ditch at Les Andalouses, to the west of Oran, on D-Day. The soldier on the left is hand-cranking a generator, while the one in the foreground is transmitting with a Morse key. Establishing contact from the beach with the task force flagship was vital to keep the commanders up to date on the status of the attack and to request fire-support missions from offshore destroyers and cruisers as well as coordinate airstrikes from carrier-borne aircraft accompanying each task force. Nonetheless, there were times, especially at the Western Task Force assault beaches on the Atlantic coast of French Morocco, when communication failures led to a delay in support and disrupted landing schedules. USAMHI

American soldiers quickly set up radio communications upon landing at one of the assault areas on November 8, 1942. This radio transmitter site is located just inland from one of the assault beaches and is partially hidden in some tall grass and local trees. Unfortunately, the tall antenna for the radio transmitter denotes its location. A soldier to the far left with his Thompson M1928 submachine gun stands by the GI hand-cranking a generator for the radio transmitter. NARA

American soldiers man both a .50-inch caliber heavy AA machine gun and a lighter .30-inch caliber Browning one in a dug-in position on the beach at Fedala, just to the north of Casablanca, after the Western Task Force disembarked its initial assault waves there. NARA

American soldiers man a 40mm Bofors AA artillery gun on an Allied assault beach soon after the landings for Operation Torch on November 8, 1942. A mounting German air presence from Tunisia and Sicily was soon to commence to resist the invasions of French Morocco and Algeria. The Swedish Bofors gun, developed in the mid-1930s, had a high rate of fire (120 rounds per minute) and was manufactured by the United States and designated the 40mm Gun M1. As shown, there was a single-barrel gun on a mobile mounting for land use, while for naval use a dual-configuration barrel was manufactured. NARA

An Allied Eastern Task Force troopship lies afire in waters off Algiers during the initial days of the invasion. The photograph was taken from the deck of an escorting Allied destroyer that would steam toward the damaged vessel to take off survivors. AUTHOR'S COLLECTION

The SS *Cathay*, a former British ocean liner but now an Allied troopship, burns after a *Luftwaffe* air attack off the port coast of Bougie, east of Algiers, on November 11, 1942. The *Cathay* was one of four infantry landing ships of the Royal Navy that was transporting the British 36th Infantry Brigade Group to Bougie. Eventually the *Cathay* and two other troopships were destroyed by the Nazi air sorties. The British 36th Infantry Brigade Group was the Eastern Task Force's floating reserve and was ordered by British First Army commander Lieutenant General Anderson to begin the attack on Bougie, 120 miles from Algiers, on the previous day, to start the eastward advance toward Tunis under orders from the Allied Forces commander, General Eisenhower. AWM

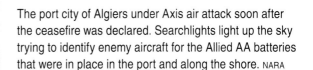

The port city of Algiers under Axis air attack soon after the ceasefire was declared. Searchlights light up the sky trying to identify enemy aircraft for the Allied AA batteries that were in place in the port and along the shore. NARA

CHAPTER 5
TUNISIAN WARFARE AND WEAPONS

After the Allied Task Forces' amphibious landings, an overland assault from Algeria was necessary to seize the Tunisian ports of Bizerte and Tunis, since the Axis air presence in Tunisia and Sicily had negated a simultaneous seaborne landing to achieve those objectives. Five German fighter groups and dive-bombers had transferred to Tunisian airfields since November 8, 1942. Although Tunisia was relatively small, extending only 160 miles east to west and 500 miles north to south, it was still more than 400 miles from Algiers, from which Lt. Gen. Kenneth Anderson's Eastern Task Force troops would have to begin their overland advance.

The overland advance was scheduled to begin on the night of November 24, and Anderson's force was made up of the British 78th Infantry Division, under the command of Maj. Gen. Vyvyan Evelegh, and an armored division, along with several smaller supporting American armor and reconnaissance contingents. This force would attack on three axes. The first objective was Tunis, followed by the encirclement of Bizerte to compel its surrender. The British troops were divided into three infantry brigade groups (IBGs). In the north, toward Bizerte, the 36th IBG would advance along a road 10 miles inland from the sea. In the south the 11th IBG would be 40 miles inland and advance in a northeasterly direction toward Tunis. A third IBG, Blade Force, would move in between the other two units, 20 miles inland, and meet with the 11th IBG near Tebourba, due west of Djedeida, for the continued eastward advance toward Tunis.

The first clash with Axis forces occurred on November 16 at Djebel Abiod, with the enemy retreating toward Bizerte after losing eight tanks. Despite this, the Allied attack commenced as scheduled. The 11th IBG was stopped at Medjez el Bab along the southern axis; however, the Germans retreated within twenty-four hours and the town of Tebourba was taken on November 27, with Axis forces withdrawing to Djedeida. Blade Force's 100 American and British tanks moved east at sunrise on November 25. The initial American-German armor engagement occurred on November 26 at Chougui, north of Tebourba, with the enemy again retreating after several tanks were knocked out on both sides. After a delay the 36th IBG started its advance on November 25–26 and ran into fixed enemy defensive positions on November 28, 30 miles to the west of Bizerte, at Djefna.

Axis defenses were stiffening, which subsequently stalled the advances of the 11th and 36th IBGs. Panzer Mk VI ("Tiger") tanks made their combat debut at Djedeida, 13 miles to the west of Tunis, proving their superiority over extant Allied armor. German air squadrons enjoyed local superiority due to hard-surface airfields east of the Atlas Mountains and more favorable weather, enabling them to attack Allied armor and infantry columns, thereby impairing their mobility, which was a factor that Eisenhower and his local commanders had counted on. Axis counteroffensives in early December from Djedeida pushed back to just east of Medjez el Bab along the southern axis while inflicting losses of roughly 500 tanks and vehicles as well as 70 artillery pieces. More than 1,000 Allied troops became prisoners of war.

Nonetheless, General Anderson planned to continue his attack on Tunis to commence on December 22, 1942. After reinforcements arrived, almost 40,000 Allied troops, now including French forces, would strike at fewer than 25,000 Axis combat troops under the command of German general Walter Nehring's XC Corps. Elements of the U.S. 1st Infantry Division and British Coldstream Guards advanced up the lower ridges of Longstop Hill, which was the dominant terrain feature controlling the river corridor to Tunis, on December 22 during heavy rain. However, on December 24, a German counterattack halted the Allied advance up the slopes, and within forty-eight hours a withdrawal was ordered, with more than 500 casualties. The Allies' highly anticipated "race for Tunis" ended in failure.

Now the Allies would have to wait for better weather since the vital need for improved air support to aid the newly formed British First Army in the north, comprising five divisions (with the British 6th Armored and 78th Infantry Divisions as the current nucleus), to fight the Axis armies had become readily apparent. Also, Maj. Gen. Lloyd R. Fredendall would command the U.S. II Corps in central Tunisia, which was to include regiments from the 1st and 2nd Armored Divisions as well as infantry from the 1st,

3rd, 9th, and 34th Divisions that moved up from their Moroccan and Algerian landing zones. Eventually the French XIX Corps, after being equipped by the Americans and under the command of Gen. Louise-Marie Koeltz, would be stationed between the British First Army and Fredendall's U.S. II Corps.

Also in December 1942, Field Marshal Albert Kesselring, commander in chief (C-in-C), South (in control of Tunisia and Rommel's Axis forces retreating through Tripolitania), activated the German 5th Panzer Army, under Gen. Hans-Jürgen von Arnim. This 5th Panzer Army would comprise the 10th Panzer Division near Tunis; an armored division under Col. Friedrich Freiherr von Broich (Division von Broich) near Bizerte; the 21st Panzer Division, under Lt. Gen. Hans-Georg Hildebrandt; the 334th Infantry Division; and the 5th Fallschirmjäger Regiment. The Italian XXX Corps would comprise the 1st Superga Division, the 47th Grenadier Regiment, and the 50th Special Brigade to the south. Eventually Rommel's *Panzer-Armee Afrika* would join von Arnim with the intent to move westward as a combined force to push the Allies back into Algeria and, perhaps, Morocco. For this operation the Axis would have to have control of the mountain passes in the Eastern and Western Dorsal Mountains of central Tunisia.

On January 30, 1943, a battle group of the German 21st Panzer Division and the Italian 50th Special Brigade, the latter with Semovente assault guns, attacked a French regiment in the Faïd Pass in the Eastern Dorsal near Sidi Bou Zid on the Sfax-Sbeitla road and defeated them there. An American counterattack with limited infantry and armor forces from Sbeitla failed to recapture the Faïd Pass and other neighboring ones, now defended by German 88mm antitank (AT) guns. Also, Fredendall's II Corps' advance during the last week of January on the Maknassy road junction via Sened—more than 30 miles to the southeast with his Combat Command C of Maj. Gen. Orlando Ward's 1st Armored Division—had to be recalled and redirected to Sidi Bou Zid instead, just to the southwest of the Faïd Pass, as a crisis was unfolding to the north.

The loss of the Faïd Pass and failed counterattacks there from January 31 to February 1 would set the stage for further German offensive movements. On February 14 columns from both the 21st and 10th Panzer Divisions, under von Arnim, with more than 200 tanks combined broke through a thin American armor defensive line at Sidi Bou Zid from two different directions. The 10th and 21st Panzer Divisions made contact with one another to the west of Sidi Bou Zid at nightfall on February 14 to consolidate their gains. A failed American armored and mechanized infantry counterattack the next day led to the capture of approximately 1,500 GIs. More than 150 American tanks, half-tracks, artillery pieces, and trucks were left on the Sidi Bou Zid battlefields. The U.S. 1st Armored Division's Combat Command A (CCA) had been crushed.

The Tunisian battlefield, mid-February 1943. After the Allies failed to win the race to Tunis in late November and December 1942, General Eisenhower called a halt to offensive operations and consolidated his forces while awaiting better weather. The British 1st Army was deployed in northern Tunisia with both armored and infantry divisions. In central and southern Tunisia, the French 19th Corps, under General Louis-Marie Koeltz, was positioned to the south of the British and to the north of the U.S. II Corps, under Maj. Gen. Lloyd Fredendall. The American II Corps comprised the 1st Armored Division, with its dispersed armored combat commands, and the 1st Infantry Division, which, likewise, had its 16th, 18th, and 26th Regiments scattered along a 200-mile front from north to south. Elements of the U.S. 34th Infantry Division were also assigned to the II Corps sector; however, their deployment was also scattered. The 5th Panzer Army, under Gen. Hans-Jürgen von Arnim, had its headquarters in Tunis; however, its infantry and armored divisions were situated along a defensive line running down the eastern side of the Eastern Dorsal Mountains from the Mediterranean coast in the north to the impassable Chott Djerid salt marshes to the south of El Guettar. Major elements of 5th Panzer Army's two panzer divisions, the 10th and the 21st, would force through the Eastern Dorsal Mountains during the second and third weeks of February, thereby preempting a U.S. II Corps offensive, which theoretically could have split the Axis forces if it reached the sea at Sfax. In addition, von Arnim's and Field Marshal Rommel's separate armored offensives inflicted major defeats on the Americans at Sidi Bou Zid and at Kasserine on February 14–15 and February 20–22, respectively. Upon entering Tunisia, Rommel's *Panzer-Armee Afrika* was situated in the south along the Mareth Line and was renamed the Italian 1st Army as major armored elements of the *Deutsches Afrikakorps* (DAK) were transferred to the German 5th Panzer Army in central Tunisia. The Italian 20th and 21st Corps, with some armor in the former, would remain in the south with elements of the DAK to combat Gen. Bernard Montgomery's advancing 8th Army from the south. MERIDIAN MAPPING

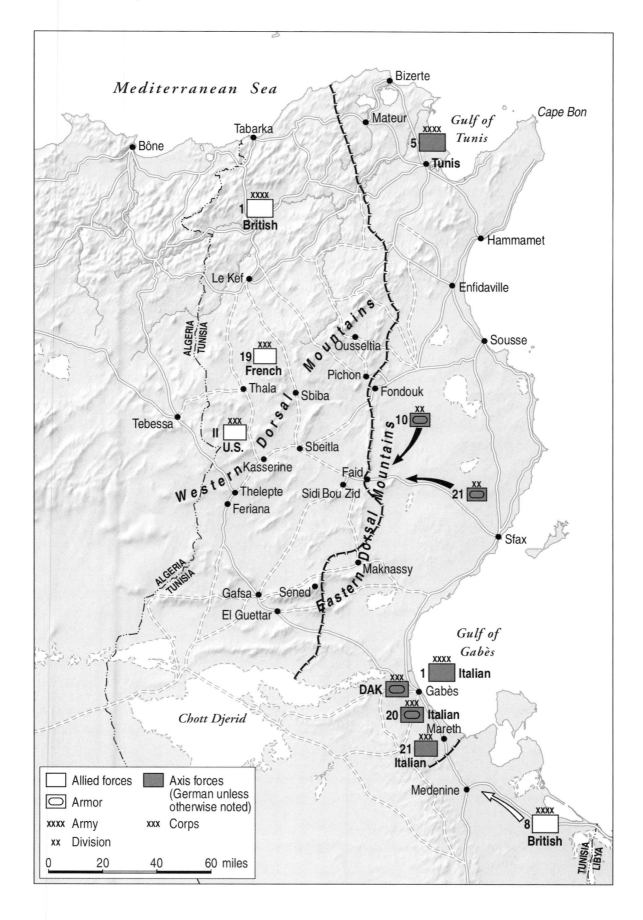

Mediterranean Sea

Bizerte

Mateur

Gulf of Tunis

Cape Bon

Tabarka

Bône

XXXX
5

Tunis

Hammamet

XXXX
1
British

Le Kef

Enfidaville

ALGERIA
TUNISIA

Sousse

XXX
19
French

Ousseltia

Pichon

Thala

Sbiba

Fondouk

XX
10

Tebessa

XXX
II
U.S.

Sbeitla

Faid

XX
21

Kasserine

Thelepte

Sidi Bou Zid

Feriana

Sfax

Maknassy

ALGERIA
TUNISIA

Gafsa

Sened

El Guettar

Gulf of Gabès

XXXX
1 **Italian**

Chott Djerid

XXX
DAK

Gabès

XXX
20 **Italian**

Mareth

XXX
21 **Italian**

Medenine

Allied forces

Axis forces
(German unless
otherwise noted)

Armor

XXXX Army

XXX Corps

XX Division

XXXX
8
British

TUNISIA
LIBYA

0   20   40   60 miles

On Kesselring's direct order, von Arnim's 21st Panzer Division continued 25 miles farther to the west, in the absence of another American counterattack, on February 16. Around Sbeitla were the remnants of the U.S. 1st Armored Division's CCA and Col. Paul Robinett's CCB. The Germans captured Sbeitla on February 17 after some lackluster fighting by the demoralized CCA, necessitating the withdrawal of CCB. The U.S. II Corps, after suffering extensive losses to the German armored thrust, had to establish a new defensive line through the Kasserine Pass, just to the southwest of Sbeitla, on the road toward Thala.

Enter Rommel! Since Gen. Bernard Montgomery's Eighth Army had outrun its supplies and needed time to reassemble its lines of communication, so Rommel strengthened the Mareth Line in southern Tunisia with his infantry (now to become the Italian First Army under General Maresciallo Giovanni Messe) and utilized the mobile elements from his retreating German-Italian panzer army to seize Gafsa and Feriana on February 17, followed by the capture of the Allied airfield at Thelepte along with many aviation stores. Meanwhile, on February 17, von Arnim sent the 10th Panzer Division north toward the Fondouk and Pinchon Passes, while leaving the 21st Panzer Division at Sbeitla. On February 18–19, Kesselring approved of Rommel's plan over von Arnim's to now attach both the 10th and 21st Panzer Divisions to Rommel in order to attack the U.S. II Corps defenses in the Kasserine Pass area on February 19. After getting through the Kasserine Pass through the Western Dorsal, Rommel could threaten Tebessa, the American supply base in Algeria on a road and railway network, and/or strike northwestward toward Thala and Le Kef, which would place him in the rear of the British First Army in northern Tunisia.

Rommel attacked the Kasserine Pass with his former *Deutsches Afrikakorps* (DAK) mechanized forces, while the 10th Panzer Division was still en route, during the early hours of February 20. The 21st Panzer Division attacked Sbiba directly due north of Sbeitla; however, this German force was repelled by Allied forces there. Initially opposing Rommel were only an American engineer regiment and a battalion of the U.S. 26th Infantry Regiment of the 1st Infantry Division. Other elements of the U.S. 39th Infantry Regiment of the 9th Infantry Division also arrived. Anderson reinforced the road to Thala by ordering in contingents of the British 26th Armoured Brigade. Late in the afternoon elements of the 10th Panzer Division (without its Mk VI Tiger tank battalion) arrived, and along with Rommel's German-Italian troops, they attacked to get through the Kasserine Pass with the intent of moving on either Thala to the northwest or Tebessa to the west. This German advance caused some Allied units to begin to retreat or become surrounded. Also, the armor of the British 26th Brigade, which had initially held off the German armor on the road to Thala, was finally overwhelmed with enemy reinforcements. Rommel's Italian tanks were moving on the road toward Tebessa. Fredendall sent in Robinett's CCB and other units of the 1st Infantry Division to block the further movement of Axis armor in light of the disintegration of Allied defensive positions.

Rommel consolidated his gains in the Kasserine Pass on February 21 as he vacillated in moving on Tebessa, Thala, or Le Kef (via Sbiba). As a result, he divided his battle groups along the three different road axes of advance, and each was to encounter increasing Allied strength. The Axis attempt to break into Thala was rebuffed by British armor; American artillery, including 105mm and 155mm howitzers of the 9th Infantry Division; and Allied fighter sorties, on the morning of February 22. American tank and artillery fire from Robinett's CCB halted the Axis movement on Tebessa on February 21. The 21st Panzer Division's movement along the road axis toward Sbiba was, likewise, stopped by British armor and American infantry defensive positions. By the afternoon of February 22, Rommel had realized that although his initial forays into the Kasserine Pass had been successful, a combination of stiffening Allied resistance along the axes of his advance, his waning fuel reserves, and the threat of Montgomery attacking the Mareth Line well to the southeast all necessitated him to issue a withdrawal order late on February 22 for all units. By the next day most of the German and Italian units had left Kasserine Pass.

After Sidi Bou Zid and Kasserine, Eisenhower altered his command structure by appointing the British general Sir Harold R.L.G. Alexander the new leader of the 18th Army Group. For the final drive to capture Tunisia, Alexander would have twenty divisions in three main groups along a front of 140 miles. The formation of a Mediterranean Air Command under British air chief marshal Sir Arthur Tedder in late February would hopefully obviate some of the inadequacies of the Allied air presence up till then. It would comprise the 242nd Royal Air Force (RAF) Group, the XII Air Support Command, and the Tactical Bomber Force. Maj. Gen. George S. Patton Jr. was to take over the command of II Corps from Fredendall, with Maj. Gen. Omar N. Bradley as his deputy.

On February 26 von Arnim launched an offensive against the British in northern Tunisia to expand his perimeter of defense for Tunis. Von Arnim's 5th Panzer Army would operate north of the area of Gabès, while Rommel would stand his forces facing southward toward Montgomery and his advancing British Eighth Army. On March 6 Rommel attacked Montgomery at Medenine; however, Eighth Army artillery and AT gunfire, along with RAF attacks on Axis columns, halted the German field marshal's last Tunisian offensive.

In mid-March the Eighth Army prepared to assault the Mareth Line with several of its divisions. The Mareth Line consisted of a series of outdated blockhouses and entrenchments built by the French in the late 1930s to protect southern Tunisia from Mussolini's Tripolitania outposts. It ran roughly from east to west halfway between Medenine to the south and Gabès to the north. The Mareth Line was to defend the plain between the Matmata Hills and the sea. To the west of the Matmata Hills were salt marshes and broken desert. Rommel harbored grave doubts about the suitability of the Mareth Line to stop Montgomery and left Africa permanently on March 9. After direct attacks on the enemy fortifications on March 20 failed, separate British operations at such locales as Wilder's and the Tebaga Gap from March 23–26 successfully turned the Mareth positions from the flank and rear, respectively. This compelled the Axis, under General Messe, to begin its retreat on March 27, first to the north of Gabès at Wadi Akarit and then farther north to Enfidaville, less than 50 miles from Tunis.

Patton's II Corps had three full infantry divisions, an armored division, and the 1st Ranger Battalion, plus engineers as well as field and coast artillery units, all totaling almost 90,000 men. In mid-March its first objective was Gafsa, directly due south of Kasserine, to draw enemy forces away from Montgomery in the south. The 1st Armored Division took Gafsa without a fight on March 17. Despite extremely muddy terrain, Sened, about 30 miles directly east of Gafsa, was captured with light opposition. The 1st Armored Division advanced an additional 20 miles to the northeast and took Maknassy uncontested. Finally, encountering stiff Axis resistance just to the east of Maknassy, the armored unit stopped its advance on March 22, just as a German counterstroke was to be unleashed on II Corps infantry at El Guettar, between Gafsa and Sened.

From March 21–24 the 1st Infantry Division repelled two major assaults by the 10th Panzer Division utilizing massed artillery, tank destroyers, mines, air sorties, and hand-to-hand combat. The American infantry suffered heavy casualties, but the Germans were compelled to withdraw. The Allied command had received their wish, namely, a diversion of Axis armor away from the Eighth Army in the south.

Following his victory at El Guettar, Patton unleashed a two-infantry-division (1st and 9th) attack to the sea between Gabès and Sfax, which would divide the Axis forces in two; however, the 9th Division, in its combat debut as a complete division, encountered stiff enemy resistance and incurred more than 1,600 casualties over nine days of combat. As little progress to the sea was made in late March and early April by II Corps, Eisenhower and Patton replaced Orlando Ward with Maj. Gen. Ernest Harmon to lead the 1st Armored Division on April 5. In any event, the Axis troops hastened in their northward retreat into the Tunis and Bizerte bridgeheads. II Corps divisions began shifting north to close in further on the two Tunisian ports.

On April 15 Bradley took command of II Corps as Patton returned to the rear echelon to plan the Sicily invasion. II Corps was to assist the British First Army in pushing back the enemy perimeter, and after the two enemy ports were isolated, Bradley was to capture Bizerte. Both the 9th Infantry Division along the coast and the 1st Infantry Division to its south had rough combat with the enemy in the hilly terrain, with daily success measured only in yards. On April 26 the 34th Infantry Division entered the II Corps thrust between the 1st and 9th Divisions. With objectives such as Hill 609 and Hill 523, the American infantry divisions continued to meet fanatical enemy resistance, with the 1st and 34th Divisions incurring more than 2,300 casualties in three days of nearly continuous combat. On April 30 II Corps began another general attack and overran Hills 609 and 523, with the Germans retreating into Mateur on the night of May 1. After two more days of tough combat, the 1st Armored Division drove the Germans out of Mateur. Bradley and his troops were only 20 miles from Bizerte.

The American attack on Bizerte with Maj. Gen. Manton S. Eddy's 9th Infantry Division and Harmon's 1st Armored Division commenced on May 6. On the next day, after some heavy street fighting in Bizerte to root out snipers with infantrymen and M3 Lee medium tanks, the retreating enemy fled through the city. Concurrent with this the British First Army's V Corps drive on Tunis began on May 3, after linking up with Eighth Army. Alexander shifted Montgomery's

7th Armored Division, the 4th Indian Division, and the 201st Guards Brigade from the Eighth Army to the First Army for this final assault on the Axis redoubt. Montgomery's remaining troops would participate only in local operations so as to conserve manpower for the upcoming Sicily invasion. Tunis fell on May 7. The Axis units encountered in and around Bizerte and Tunis were in a state of complete disarray, with wholesale surrender commonplace. Eventually 275,000 Axis prisoners surrendered with the capture of Bizerte and Tunis. With the advent of the second week of May, the hard-fought, six-month-long Tunisian campaign was over, with the formal Axis surrender on May 13, 1943.

A column of combat equipment–laden American infantry marches in single file along a desert track punctuated with small rocks and sparse vegetation growth. Towering above the desert floor are the Dorsal Mountains of Tunisia, with their passes, such as at Faïd and Kasserine, each of which had high strategic value. The disposition of the column is to minimize casualties if any Axis artillery were fired on it. NARA

Infantrymen of the 9th Division, under the command of Maj. Gen. Manton Eddy, crouch with full combat packs amid some of the ruins of Bizerte on May 7, 1943. Sporadic German sniper fire was a continual hazard, and the enemy had to be cleared one house at a time. This combat often involved an M3 medium Lee tank (far background) being employed to use its array of heavy weapons on the dwelling after infantry located Nazi snipers. NARA

A column of the Durham Light Infantry marches along a Tunisian road in pairs, dutifully following a sapper with a metallic mine detector. Both combatant sides sowed antipersonnel mines on and along roads to delay the advancing enemy infantry. This British Eighth Army infantry column was advancing on El Hamma near the Axis Mareth Line in southeastern Tunisia and the road to Gabès in late March 1943. The Axis positions at El Hamma included elements of the German 15th and 21st Panzer Divisions of *Deutsches Afrikakorps* fame. AWM

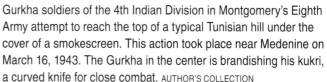

Gurkha soldiers of the 4th Indian Division in Montgomery's Eighth Army attempt to reach the top of a typical Tunisian hill under the cover of a smokescreen. This action took place near Medenine on March 16, 1943. The Gurkha in the center is brandishing his kukri, a curved knife for close combat. AUTHOR'S COLLECTION

British infantrymen of the 7th Rifle Brigade charge across an open field against German defensive works, which are, in fact, ruined houses in the Kounine Hills, in April 1943 during Montgomery's Eighth Army advance toward Tunis from southern Tunisia. The 7th Rifle Brigade was part of the 7th Motor Brigade within Montgomery's 1st Armoured Division, which fought as part of X Corps. NARA

An American tank destroyer crewman with an M1928 Thompson submachine gun races after fleeing crew members of an abandoned Axis antitank (AT) gun that was situated in a dug-in position in the Tunisian desert near El Guettar in late March 1943. Other mechanized vehicles can be seen in the background. NARA

American private Aloysius Unsen (left) and a British First Army soldier, Taffy Morgan (right), take cover in the midst of enemy sniper fire in Tunis on May 7, 1943. Both Allied soldiers are armed with M1928 Thompson submachine guns. The fighting for Tunis was nearing its end by this time. NARA

A Royal Engineer lifts a mine out of its buried place after the detonating device had been removed. The mine was laid on the Thala-Kasserine Road during Rommel's withdrawal after his offensive to the north and west of the Kasserine Pass became stalled with stiffening Allied resistance on February 20–22, 1943. The retreating German troops planted tens of thousands of antivehicle and antipersonnel mines to slow down the Allied pursuit. AUTHOR'S COLLECTION

An Italian Bersaglieri machine-gunner fires at a house in Tunisia while the crew member to the left acts as a spotter. The weapon mounted on a tripod is probably a Breda 37 heavy machine gun. The Bersaglieri were initially formed in the nineteenth century and were skilled sharpshooters. During the North African campaign, the Bersaglieri battalions were an elite corps of light infantry, which achieved notable successes in Tunisia with Rommel at the Kasserine Pass on February 20–23, 1943, along with the capture of hundreds of British paratroopers on December 5, 1942, south of Tunis during an abortive British Airborne assault to capture airfields near the port. Members of the battalions were volunteers who were hand-picked on the basis of their physical courage and condition, as well as being better-educated troops in the Italian Army. NARA

A young German paratrooper in Tunisia is fully equipped with his rifle, pistol, stick hand grenade, and extra belts of ammunition draped around his neck. By D-Day plus two German paratroopers of the 5th Parachute Regiment began to arrive in Tunisia in strength. The German paratroops were noted for their ferocity and tenacious defense when employed as light infantry throughout the entire war. AUTHOR'S COLLECTION

A dead German soldier lies sprawled across the *Nebelwerfer* that he was manning in the hills near Tunis. The *Nebelwerfer* 41 was a relatively new weapon when it was employed in Tunisia. It was a 150mm, six-barreled rocket launcher patterned on a similar Russian weapon. The *Nebelwerfer* soon received the moniker "Screaming Meemie" by the Allies due to the high-pitched, shrill sound it made, which could instill great fear in the Allies on the receiving end. AUTHOR'S COLLECTION

A French colonial bunker on the Mareth Line covering the main road that crosses over the Wadi Zigzaou, from which Montgomery's British 50th Division forces were planning to attack the defensive works. AUTHOR'S COLLECTION

Members of the 1st Battalion of the 51st Scottish Highland Division (Black Watch) inspect the contents of a Mareth Line bunker and trench that they just captured from the enemy in March 1943. AWM

British soldiers of the 7th Rifle Brigade from X Corps' 7th Motor Brigade defend a position consisting of a chest-high stone wall that they just captured from the enemy in the Kounine hills during Eighth's Army advance toward Tunis in April 1943. USAMHI

A pair of American-built M3 light Stuart tanks races across the flat, featureless desert as part of the 8th King's Royal Irish Hussars. Liked by the British early in the North African campaign for its mechanical reliability and high speed, this tank was woefully obsolete by the time of Operation Torch since it had a limited range; it was undergunned, with its main armament being a 37mm turret gun; and its armor protection was too thin. Also, its high-octane gasoline engine made it very vulnerable to being set ablaze by enemy fire. NARA

An M3 light Stuart tank commander sits atop his tank turret peering for Axis armor across the rocky, scrub Tunisian desert floor, with the usual djebels in the background. Due to the unfavorable features of the M3 light tank at the time of Operation Torch, this type of tank was often relegated to a reconnaissance role. NARA

An American M5 light tank in Oran in 1943 as it is prepared for the fighting in Tunisia. This tank still had the 37mm main turret gun along with three .30-inch caliber Browning machine guns. Some M5 light tanks of the U.S. 70th Battalion were landed by the Western Task Force in early November 1942 and saw action near Casablanca, as most of the landing craft available for Operation Torch were inadequate for disembarking medium tanks in the first waves, and as a result they could only be landed after ports with dock facilities were captured. However, after combat with the German panzers as well as their 50mm PaK 38 and 75mm PaK 40 AT guns, it was apparent that the M5's 37mm gun was outranged and its armor too thin to withstand the armor-piercing shells of the enemy guns. As a result, both the M3 and M5 would be used only for reconnaissance and flank security. NARA

An American tanker in Tunisia cleans the barrel of his M3 medium Lee tank's main 75mm sponson-mounted gun. The M3 medium tank was hurriedly produced in 1941 as there was a compelling need for such an armored fighting vehicle in both the American and British forces. The M3 tank's sponson-mounted 75mm gun was capable of firing high-explosive and armor-piercing rounds as did the turret mounted 37mm dual-purpose gun. The reason for mounting the heavier weapon in the sponson was related to the inexperience of tank designers and manufacturers in 1940 in producing the proper turret, turret ring, and gun mount for the 75mm gun. NARA

An M3 medium Lee tank rounds a corner in battle-scarred Bizerte in May 1943 while two others trail behind. An infantryman from the U.S. 9th Infantry Division lies prone after German sniper fire was encountered. During November and December 1942, the single battalion of M3 medium Lee tanks in the U.S. 1st Armored Division also saw extensive action, initially against Vichy French forces after the amphibious landings and then against German panzers on the road to Mateur while supporting British infantry. During this initial combat in Tunisia, Combat Command B of the 1st Armored Division lost 40 M3 medium Lee tanks, as they were no match for the German Mk IV panzers. USAMHI

A disabled M3 medium Lee tank stands abandoned with one of its crew lying dead by its side at Sened Station, halfway between Gafsa and Maknassy. This locale was the site of a raid in late January 1943 and was part of the II Corps counterattack in March 1943 after the disasters at Faïd and Kasserine Passes. USAMHI

An M4 medium Sherman tank with its 75mm turret gun in Tunisia, 1943. The 1st Armored Division sailed to North Africa with the older M3 medium Lee tanks in its medium tank battalions, while the 2nd Armored Division, which landed in Morocco, received the available M4 medium tanks. The rationale for keeping the 2nd Armored Division in Morocco was largely logistic, as there were limits to the railway line to Tebessa and American trucks were breaking down, with no new ones expected until well into 1943. Also, some of the Allied Headquarters commanders remained unduly fearful of an Axis strike through Spain. As the campaign wore on, more M4 medium tanks arrived on the Tunisian front. USAMHI

An M4A1 medium Sherman tank, with its commander scanning for Axis armor from his top turret hatch into the distance in the vicinity of Kasserine Pass in late February 1943. The better-equipped U.S. 2nd Armored Division, with the M4 medium Sherman tanks, ironically saw little fighting after the initial Torch landings and remained in Morocco with Generals Patton and Harmon, while the 1st Armored Division did the bulk of the initial combat in Tunisia in November and December 1942 with the more obsolete M3 medium Lee tanks. NARA

M4 medium Sherman tanks in British service battle with Axis forces along the outskirts of Tunis in May 1943. In the summer of 1942, the 2nd Armored Division, which had received the initial production of the Sherman tanks, had to relinquish these new armored vehicles for subsequent use by Montgomery's Eighth Army in the Second Battle of El Alamein, which commenced on October 23, 1942. The newly arrived M4 medium Sherman tanks contributed greatly to Montgomery's success, as they outperformed the Eighth Army's M3 medium Grant and near obsolete Crusader tanks. AWM

A pair of M10 3-inch gun motor carriages (GMC), or tank destroyers, with their turret guns depressed and facing rearward, passes by an Arab village in Tunisia. The M10 saw its combat debut in Tunisia in March 1943 with newly arrived tank battalions. The M10 3-inch GMC was basically an M4A2 medium tank chassis mounting a 3-inch gun in an open turret. It was a marked improvement over the M3 half-track-mounted armored vehicles and became the standard tank destroyer throughout Tunisia and into the Italian campaign. Although it had slightly better firepower, it had much less armor that the M4 medium Sherman tank. The M10 3-inch GMC played a decisive role in stopping elements of the 10th Panzer Division at El Guettar on March 23, 1943. NARA

American soldiers of the 1st Armored Division are seen in Tunisia in December 1942 in an early production of an M7 105mm howitzer motor carriage called a "Priest." This self-propelled artillery piece was built on the M3 medium tank chassis. During the war the M7 incorporated many of the features of the M4 medium Sherman tank and saw extensive action as one of the better self-propelled artillery pieces that the Allies fielded. NARA

An M3 half-track 75mm GMC. This was the primary American heavy tank destroyer fighting in Tunisia after the landings on November 8, 1942. The M3 75mm GMC suffered from a very limited traverse, and its cross-country speed was deemed inadequate. The 75mm gun was of World War I vintage, utilizing the French M1897 design. This GMC was a hasty improvement over the M6 37mm GMC and had some success at El Guettar in March 1943 against elements of the 10th Panzer Division; however, many were destroyed by German tank fire in that battle. Army Ordnance finally developed the M10 GMC, which arrived in Tunisia for combat in March 1943. NARA

A light tank destroyer, the M6 37mm GMC. It was a hasty improvisation created by mounting the 37mm gun in the rear of a three-quarter-ton truck. Unfortunately, this motorized AT weapon offered little armored protection for its crew; it had poor cross-country performance; and its gun traverse was limited to the rear. Furthermore, the 37mm gun lacked the firepower to deal with German tanks and the rear bed of the truck prohibited adequate servicing of the weapon. The M6 37mm GMC was removed from tank destroyer units whenever feasible and replaced with the M3 75mm GMC using a half-track as the armored vehicle. AUTHOR'S COLLECTION

Two officers (foreground) of the U.S. 601st Tank Destroyer Battalion pore over a map in front of their M3 command half-track at El Guettar in late March 1943. Two jeeps and an M3 75mm GMC tank destroyer are to the rear of this reconnaissance half-track. At El Guettar the M3 75mm GMC tank destroyer played a pivotal role in halting the advance of a 10th Panzer Division battle group. NARA

A reconnaissance half-track radios in Axis movements to rear echelon headquarters. Many radio antennae can be seen on this vehicle, as well as a .50-inch caliber Browning heavy machine gun on a mounting for defense against Axis aerial attack. NARA

American soldiers in the multipurpose Willys jeep tow a 37mm AT gun over some rough terrain in Tunisia. A small hill, or djebel, characteristic of the Tunisian terrain is in the background. Although this was an expedient way to get the AT gun into position against a mobile enemy, the gun's performance against German armor was poor. NARA

An M3A1 scout car, with a forward-facing .30-inch caliber Browning light machine gun, advances forward as a reconnaissance vehicle for the U.S. 9th Infantry Division, roughly 15 miles from Bizerte, in early May 1943. NARA

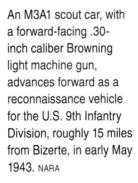

A reconnaissance jeep with its three crew members who survived the fighting at Sidi Bou Zid in mid-February. The vehicle and crew were surrounded on Djebel Lessouda by von Arnim's panzer forces for three days before making their escape on February 17, 1943. NARA

An American machine gun crew with a twin .50-inch caliber Browning machine gun mounted in the rear bed of a three-quarter-ton truck remains on alert in a dug-in position at El Guettar on March 23, 1943. This vehicle could be used to fend off low-flying Axis fighter-bombers supporting the German 10th Panzer Division assault or be trained in attacking Axis infantry. USAMHI

A pair of American soldiers in a reconnaissance jeep uses a radio telephone to direct artillery rounds at El Guettar on March 23, 1943. For defense the jeep has a rear-mounted .30-inch caliber Browning light machine gun on an aerial monopod. The uneven paint markings on the vehicle and driver's helmet might be for camouflage purposes.
NARA

An American artillery piece commander receives map coordinates and other instruction from his forward observers and passes these on to the gun's crew to make the necessary adjustment. The artillery piece is not visible but is camouflaged by netting with hessian strips.
NARA

An American artilleryman sets the fuse on a 155mm high-explosive shell after instructions have been given by the gun's commander after input from forward observers communicating with the rear via radio and telephone. NARA

A 155mm "Long Tom" cannon under its camouflage netting fires its round during a mission that was coordinated through the forward reconnaissance team to the gun commander and finally to its crew for the appropriate shell and gun settings. This gun was the most important weapon in the American long-range artillery inventory. Its specifically designed carriage enabled it to move across country. With its maximum range at just over 25,000 yards and it rate of fire of one round per minute, it could defeat any other piece of heavy artillery and was excellent for counterbattery fire and against remote fixed enemy positions. NARA

During action at El Guettar on March 23, 1943, General Patton employed a wide array of AT and heavier artillery pieces to disrupt the German infantry formations accompanying the elements of the 10th Panzer Division. This gun crew is firing a M1918 155mm howitzer on an M1918A3 carriage that was older equipment based on a similar artillery piece of French design used in WWI. USAMHI

An American crew has set up their 105mm M2A1 howitzer mounted in the rear of an M3 half-track to fire on 10th Panzer Division tanks at El Guettar on March 23, 1943, in an effort to stem the Axis advance. This was the primary weapon of the American artillery units, but here it is being used in an AT role. The design of this howitzer was completed in 1939, and it entered production the following year. Firing a high-explosive shell, the gun's maximal range was just over 12,000 yards. NARA

The crew of an American 105mm M2A1 howitzer readies a shell to fire in support of the defense at Kasserine Pass in late February 1943. This gun and crew were part of the 33rd Field Artillery Battalion of the 1st Infantry Division. The crew is utilizing the remains of an Arab mud brick house for concealment. One disadvantage of this excellent artillery piece was that its weight of almost 5,000 pounds for its caliber limited its towing and positioning to a two-and-a-half-ton truck. NARA

An American infantry gun crew has set their M3 37mm AT gun on the Tunisian desert floor on February 14, 1943, near Sidi Bou Zid in response to General von Arnim's breakthrough via the Faïd Pass during the Axis counteroffensive. The gun weighed just over 900 pounds in the firing position, so it was easy to tow and move from position to position; however, its armor-piercing rounds, which were effective against Vichy French and thinly armored Italian armored vehicles, were no match for the German Mk III and Mk IV panzers that were employed against the Allies. In the background is Djebel Lessouda, where an American infantry battalion was surrounded by the advancing Axis forces. NARA

An American M3 37mm AT gun crew watches for attacking Axis armor from a minimally concealed position on typical Tunisian rock-strewn desert mixed with scrub as the battle at Sidi Bou Zid was about to erupt on February 14, 1943. During von Arnim's counteroffensive the Americans around Sidi Bou Zid lost more than fifty-five half-tracks, twenty-five artillery pieces, and twenty trucks due to poor deployment and lack of suitable cover. The 37mm AT gun was woefully inadequate against German armor at this stage of the war. NARA

To defend against the sorties flown by the *Luftwaffe* in support of the 10th Panzer Division's battle group thrust at El Guettar on March 23, 1943, a 40mm Bofors M1 antiaircraft (AA) gun was deployed there. This fine weapon was originally designed for the Swedish Navy and was subsequently manufactured under licensing agreements by several combatant and noncombatant nations. The crew attempted to have somewhat of a dug-in position on the hard, rock-laden Tunisian desert floor with sandbags placed on the lip of the entrenchment. Approximately 2,000 pounds in weight, this AA gun, although vehicle-towed, was highly mobile. USAMHI

An American mortarman in Tunisia sights and adjusts his 81mm mortar. The 81mm mortar was the largest weapon in the U.S. Army's infantry battalion arsenal, enabling the regimental subunit with a means to provide rapid and heavy indirect fire on enemy positions. NARA

Three members of a U.S. Army battalion's 81mm mortar team in a recessed area of a Tunisian hillside. Given that the mortar could fire at high angles to break up enemy formations, the positioning of this weapon offers some protection to the crew but might require a forward observer or utilizing known map coordinates if direct visual contact was not operant. NARA

A German Panzer II light tank that was captured in the Libyan desert by British forces. The first production of this light tank commenced in 1935 as overt German tank development was delayed by Allied enforcement of the conditions of the Versailles Treaty. Successive models of this tank differed only in the thickness of the armor, with the Panzer II being the armored spearhead of the blitzkriegs in Poland and the West in September 1939 and May 1940, respectively. With the onset of North African combat in February and March 1941, it was becoming obsolete. With a crew of three and being undergunned with one 20mm cannon and one machine gun, it was used mostly for reconnaissance. AWM

A German Panzer III medium tank, knocked out in the Western Desert, is identified in profile by its six bogey wheels. Its production began in 1939, and it saw action in Poland and France. The Panzer III shown had a 50mm main turret gun, a crew of five, and was the Germans' main battle tank in the desert conflict through 1942. AWM

Destroyed later-model German Panzer III tanks remain abandoned in the Tunisian hills north of Medenine in March 1943. These tanks carried a long-barreled, highly effective main 50mm L/42 turret gun along with a 7.92mm machine gun and had a crew of five. Production of the later Panzer III models ended in 1943 as the *Wehrmacht* moved to production of heavier tanks, principally to compete on the Russian front. AUTHOR'S COLLECTION

A burning German Panzer IV medium tank in profile, with its 75mm KwK short-barreled turret gun. The Panzer IV is identified by its eight bogey wheels. Production of the tank started in 1934 and continued through the end of the war, with the reliable chassis being used for a number of German armored vehicle variants. AWM

The American assistant secretary of war, John McCloy, inspects a disabled Panzer IV medium tank in Tunisia in the spring of 1943. A characteristic Tunisian djebel, or hill, is in the background. Both the tank's tread and a bogey wheel have been knocked off the chassis, probably by a land mine. NARA

American infantrymen look over a German Panzer IV that was disabled during the II Corps counteroffensive in late February and early March after the dual disasters at Sidi Bou Zid and Kasserine Pass on February 14 and February 20, 1943, respectively. A longer main 75mm turret gun than the short-barreled earlier model one is evident. NARA

A later-model Panzer IV medium tank (probably Ausf. H version), with its much longer gun and muzzle brake, is shown in profile. This tank was disabled in the II Corps drive through the Tunisian hills in April 1943 as part of General Bradley's plan to capture Bizerte. NARA

A Panzer V heavy "Panther" that was captured by the British in Tunisia has some British officers sitting and posing atop its turret. The Panzer V was considered to be one of the best tanks of WWII and was specifically designed to combat Soviet tanks that had outclassed the Panzer IV medium tanks on the Russian front in 1942. Early prototypes were completed in September 1942 for limited combat in Tunisia in the spring of 1943 and in larger numbers for the major tank conflagration at Kursk in July 1943. In contrast to the Panzer IV medium tank's weight of 55,000 pounds, the Panther weighed more than 100,000 pounds and had one 75mm turret gun and three 7.92mm machine guns.
AUTHOR'S COLLECTION

A German Panzer VI heavy "Tiger" on the move down the face of a Tunisian hill. The Tiger went into production in August 1942, and a total of roughly 1,300 of this early version were produced before the Tiger II (King Tiger) replaced it during the spring of 1944. The Panzer VI made its combat debut in Tunisia in late 1942. Its intricate design limited production, and maintenance was always a large issue. In the tank's semiprofile in the photograph, the overlapping wheel suspension is evident, which could contribute to mechanical difficulties with terrain debris. Its firepower was enormous, with one 88mm KwK 36 turret gun and one 7.92mm MG 34 machine gun, which can be seen on the left side of the forward portion of the hull. The Panzer VI had a crew of five. AUTHOR'S COLLECTION

A German Panzer VI heavy Tiger tank sits disabled in the Tunisian desert. Armor-piercing entry sites for rounds fired by Allied tanks appear to both the left and right of the German cross emblem on the hull. The overlapping wheel suspension is more apparent in this view. Elements of two battalions of Panzer VI tanks were shipped from Sicily to Tunisia after the Torch landings on November 8, 1942; however; their numbers were too few to be of major assistance to the Axis defense. USAMHI

A German 150mm sFH 12/1 auf Geschützwagen, or "Lorraine Schlepper" self-propelled gun, lies abandoned in the desert during a retreat. The 150mm sFH gun was the standard *Wehrmacht* heavy field howitzer. This tracked heavy artillery piece was one of many 105–150mm gun hybrids built on the Panzer Mk III and IV chassis. The chassis for this piece of German ordnance is a Mk III Panzer hull. AWM

With the initial lightning successes in the Soviet Union in 1941, large numbers of the Russian 76.2mm field artillery divisional gun were captured and removed to Germany. Here is a German *Sd.Kfz.* 139 Marder III, which was a hybrid of the Russian M1936 76.2mm gun mounted on a captured Czechoslovakian T38 tank hull. Both the top and the back were unprotected, leaving the crew exposed; however, this self-propelled artillery piece had the dual advantage of being very fast and having a powerful gun. In addition to being a powerful field artillery piece, the Russian 76.2mm gun when unmounted was one of the more effective AT weapons utilized by the Nazis in North Africa. AWM

A wrecked German *Kfz.* 15 staff car lies abandoned near Bizerte in late April or early May 1943. Many German officers, including Rommel, would frequently be seen at the front in vehicles such as these to exhort their troops and armored vehicles forward. USAMHI

A German *Sd.Kfz.* 9 18-ton heavy half-track called a FAMO is inspected by Allied soldiers after being abandoned in the desert after an Allied fighter-bomber attack at El Hamma near the Mareth Line. The FAMO was by far the largest of all half-tracks fielded during WWII by any combatant nation. The conception for such a tracked vehicle began in 1936 when it was linked to the need for a heavy recovery/towing vehicle for heavy artillery units. It had a crew of nine and weighed almost 40,000 pounds. AWM

A German 88mm AT/AA gun is towed by a *Sd.Kfz.* 9 in the Tunisian desert. This weapon-carrying version was produced in 1943 for the 88mm gun. A gun crew of up to nine would ride in the FAMO to service the gun when deployed for combat. The Mk VI Tiger tank was so large that it required two *Sd.Kfz.* 9s to recover it after disabling or mechanical failure. AWM

A German gun crew fires their 88mm FLAK AA gun in an AT role in Tunisia. An 88mm FLAK 18 was originally developed in 1933, and subsequent designs (FLAK 36 and 37) improved on barrel design and fire-control data transmission, respectively. The FLAK 18 weighed almost 5 tons, necessitating a tractor or FAMO to move it, and had a crew of nine men. A major advantage of this gun in either AA or AT roles was its high rate of fire of twenty-five rounds per minute with accuracy against moving targets. AUTHOR'S COLLECTION

A pair of captured German 88mm FLAK 18 AA/AT guns in a fixed position with their wheels detached. Although it was devastating against Allied armor when tactically deployed in an AT role, a weakness of this gun was its inability to place accurate fire on diving fighter-bombers. Although not shown with these two guns, gun shields were employed at times to protect the crew of nine, as well as having the guns set in dug-in positions. NARA

A German 88mm FLAK gun deployed in a static role in Tunisia lies destroyed by Allied armor in a relatively unprotected position at Kairouan. Some dead members of the gun crew lie beside their artillery piece. AWM

American soldiers view a German 75mm PaK 40 AT gun that was captured at Sidi Bou Zid after the Allied counteroffensive to recover from the disaster that had previously occurred there in mid-February 1943. The German AT gun, partially concealed in desert cactus, made its combat debut in Tunisia and easily outclassed the American 37mm AT gun. USAMHI

Rear view of a destroyed German 75mm PaK 40 AT gun at the battle for Sened Station in March 1943. The successful American attack was made by elements of the U.S. 1st Armored Division's Combat Command A advancing along the Gafsa road accompanied by infantrymen of the U.S. 9th Division. A number of American tanks were disabled by German AT guns deployed in concealed positions such as these. NARA

The barrel of a German field gun has been entirely destroyed by Allied armor near Maknassy during II Corps' counteroffensive during late March 1943 in Tunisia after the disastrous battles of mid- to late February 1943 brought on by Generals von Arnim and Rommel's attacks. NARA

A captured German 50mm PaK 38 field artillery piece that could also be used in an AT role, shown in profile. Its long barrel and muzzle brake yield a high muzzle velocity. It was one of Germany's most useful and reliable weapons throughout the war; however, as larger-caliber *Wehrmacht* AT guns were desirable to combat improving Allied tanks, the 75mm PaK 40 AT gun appeared in Tunisia. AWM

A German 37mm AA gun, the FLAK 43, sits in the Tunisian desert with its wheels detached. It was captured during the Allied advance during the spring of 1943. Like the 40mm Bofors gun, it had a high rate of fire and was capable of deterring low-level Allied air attacks on tanks and infantry formations. NARA

A German 20mm FLAK 38 AA gun with three cannons mounted with a gun shield. Two- and four-cannon variants also existed. These AA guns were the standard German weapons against low-flying Allied aircraft. NARA

An Italian Carro Armato M13/40 medium tank that was captured in the Tunisian desert. The tank was slow and underpowered, yet it was the principal Italian tank of the war in North Africa. Its 47mm main turret gun fired armor-piercing rounds and was effective against British tanks, utilizing a 2-pounder solid-shot turret gun. Eventually, as newer Allied tanks became available, the M13/40 was unable to perform well. NARA

An Italian Semovente M41 75/18 self-propelled turretless 75mm gun mounted on an M40 chassis lies disabled in the rough scrub country in the vicinity of Sened Station in March 1943. With its short 75mm gun, this was one of the best Italian armored vehicles that fought the Allies in Tunisia. NARA

An Italian artillery crew man a 75mm field howitzer in a partially dug-in position. As a military arm, the Italian artillery were known for their bravery throughout the North African conflict, often fighting with both inferior equipment and motorized capability to adapt to the tactical situation or mount an effective retreat. NARA

A captured Italian 104/32 Model 15 cannon on the Tunisian desert floor. It was produced on a Skoda (in Pilsen, Czechoslovakia) armaments design for the Austro-Hungarian army of WWI, exemplifying the antiquated state of the Italian artillery arm in North Africa. NARA

A British 4.5-inch gun of the 64th Medium Regiment, Royal Artillery, fighting alongside Montgomery's Eighth Army, bombards Axis positions on the Mareth Line in southern Tunisia. These guns could be mobile for bombardment or installed in stationary fortifications for use as AA weapons. AUTHOR'S COLLECTION

A British Ordnance QF 17-pounder (76.2mm) AT gun in action near Medenine in southern Tunisia as part of Montgomery's Eighth Army advance in March 1943. The gun was introduced as a prototype in August 1942 and was rapidly deployed to North Africa to deal with the threat of the German Mk VI Tiger tanks. The gun utilized the carriage of the British 25-pounder and was easily handled by its crew of seven, with a rate of fire of up to ten rounds per minute. In regard to its use against the German Mk VI panzers, the 17-pounder's round could pierce just over 5 inches of armor plating at a 1,000-yard distance. AUTHOR'S COLLECTION

A British Universal, or Bren, Carrier enters the town of Mareth, situated between Medenine to the south and Gabès to the north, in southern Tunisia. The term "Universal" applied to the carrier was apt since it could be used for a variety of combat functions, from simply moving infantry to being armed with a Bren light machine gun, a Boys AT rifle, and a mortar. NARA

A British Humber armored scout car of the 4th Light Armoured Brigade stands in bivouac in northern Tunisia, with olive trees in the background. The Humber, from a numerical standpoint, was one of the most important armored cars in British service, with more than 5,000 having been produced. In this photograph the Humber armored car carries one 15mm gun and an adjacent 7.92mm Besa machine gun. NARA

A Marmon-Herrington armored car being serviced on a Tunisian road. These armored cars were assembled in South Africa from a multitude of foreign parts. The vehicle had a reputation for being rugged and easy to maintain under the difficult terrain conditions of North Africa. The weaponry was highly individualized among these armored cars. NARA

A British Daimler scout car is utilized as a site for an impromptu review of map coordinates in preparation for the advance on Tunis by elements of the British Eighth Army on May 7, 1943. This armored car was initially developed in the late 1930s for reconnaissance purposes, with speed, especially in reverse, to compensate for a lack of heavy armament or armor plating. AWM

A British Infantry Tank Mk IV, dubbed the Churchill, leads supporting British infantry through a grassy field near Medjez el Bab in late April 1943. These tanks met with disaster at the Dieppe assault of August 1942, and literally only a handful of these heavier tanks were employed during the Second Battle of El Alamein in October and November 1942. Their numbers increased appreciably for mobility across the rugged Tunisian terrain and to effectively compete with the German Mk VI Tiger tanks utilizing their 6-pounder turret guns. The Churchill tank had a crew of five, and several variants were produced using its chassis throughout the war. AUTHOR'S COLLECTION

An RAF Supermarine Spitfire Mk V is shown here on takeoff from Souk el Khemis in Tunisia in March 1943. Design on the generic fighter began in the mid-1930s. This model was fitted with 250-pound bombs on shackles on the underwings. The Mk V had a strengthened fuselage for the bomb load as well as for a fuel drop tank to extend its range. AUTHOR'S COLLECTION

A U.S. Army Air Forces (USAAF) B-17 Flying Fortress four-engine bomber, which was crashed into by a Nazi fighter in the rear of its fuselage. The B-17, capable of taking incredible punishment, managed to limp home to its airfield in Algeria. The rear machine gun in the tail identifies this as a later model, probably a B-17F, with a design that was further refining defensive armament against nose or tail enemy fighter attacks. USAMHI

A flight of North American B-25 Mitchell twin-engine bombers fly low over the Mediterranean Sea on one of their many sorties in February 1943. The B-25 entered service in 1942 and was made famous by its use in the Doolittle Raid on Tokyo in April of that year, when sixteen of these aircraft lifted off from the USS *Hornet* in the northern Pacific. In addition to its array of machine guns and cannon variants, this plane could deliver a 3,000-pound bomb or torpedo load. USAMHI

A British Douglas A-20 Boston Mk III bomber attacks enemy tank units on Djebel bou Louron in March 1943. These aircraft were manufactured in the United States and taken over by the British from French contracts. They initially entered combat in October 1941. An Mk III model with four 20mm nose cannons was given the name Intruder, while the American version of the A-20 was called the Havoc. AUTHOR'S COLLECTION

A flight of the Douglas C-47 Skytrain (USAAF) aircraft, also known as the R4D (U.S. Navy and Marine Corps) or Dakota (to the British), flies low over the Mediterranean Sea in preparation for a paratroop drop in Tunisia to seize airfields in the early aftermath of the amphibious invasion. In addition to carrying paratroops in all theaters, these transport aircraft could also tow gliders for airborne assaults. More than 10,000 of these pivotal transport aircraft were produced during the war. USAMHI

Three Ju 87 *Luftwaffe* dive-bombers, or *Sturzkampfflugzeugs* (*Stukas*), prepare to attack Allied shipping in the landing zones and principal North African ports. This single-engine, two-seat plane was standard equipment in the *Luftwaffe* and gave Axis ground forces fighting in North Africa an "aerial umbrella" of close air support. Due to the characteristics of its steep dive and slow air speed (238 mph), it was vulnerable to Allied AA weaponry of all sorts and to fighter attack. Its inverted gull wings and massive nonretractable landing gear gave it a characteristic appearance in flight, which, along with its dive trumpets, terrified recipients of a dive-bombing with its bomb load of over 1,000 kilograms. AUTHOR'S COLLECTION

A British Eighth Army truck column is halted, with some vehicles in flames and smoke after a Ju-87 *Stuka* dive-bombing attack on the Gabès Road near El Hamma on April 1, 1943. British soldiers mill around an M3 medium Grant tank that was untouched in the air attack. AUTHOR'S COLLECTION

A *Luftwaffe* Focke-Wulf 190A captured intact in Tunisia. The American soldiers near the plane are examining it within its revetment, despite previous Allied air sorties against Axis airfields near Tunis. This fighter was the only German one to enter large-scale production and combat during the course of the conflict. The single-seat Fw 190A, with a maximum speed of just under 400 mph, made its combat debut in the fall of 1941 during the waning weeks of the daytime assault on England. Numerous upgrades were to follow. Its armament comprised four 20mm fixed forward-firing cannons in the wings and two 7.92mm forward-firing machine guns in the forward fuselage. The extensive network of Axis airdromes in both Tunisia and Sicily gave far-reaching aerial support to Axis ground forces in North Africa and the competitive edge in the first few months after the invasion in November 1942. USAMHI

A bomb-damaged Axis airfield near Tunis toward the end of the campaign. However, a Ju-88 twin-engine, four-seat bomber remains intact to the left, with an Fw 190A to the right. This plane was developed in the mid-1930s and underwent numerous modifications during the war in an attempt to compete with the high-speed British Mosquito. Its roles were varied, after it proved vulnerable to RAF fighter attack during the Battle of Britain, and included reconnaissance and night-fighting. It had extremely good armament, with an array of six 20mm cannons and a 13mm machine gun in the rear of the cockpit. USAMHI

An eighteen-passenger, three-engine Ju-52 transport lies wrecked in a Tunisian field. By the start of the war, it was obsolete as a bomber, but it served throughout the war as the backbone of the *Luftwaffe*'s transport fleet to airdrop paratroops as well as air-land reinforcements and supplies. It did have three machine guns for defense, but its speed of approximately 190 mph necessitated fighter protection to complete its missions. After the Allied landings on November 8, 1942, these transport planes essentially ran a shuttle service from the Italian mainland and Sicily, bringing troops to Tunisia at the rate of 1,000 men per day to strengthen the bridgehead there and eventually mount a defense west of Bizerte and Tunis. USAMHI

CHAPTER 6
EPILOGUE

The fighting in Tunisia, after the relatively uncontested amphibious landings in French Morocco and Algeria during Operation Torch on November 8, 1942, had brought the Allied High Command to a sobering assessment that fighting Nazi Germany would be difficult, as evidenced by the need for six months to capture Tunisia from a starting point of Algiers. The original aims of the campaign, after the landings, were to be in Tunis by Christmas and to finally trap Rommel ("the Desert Fox") with his retreating panzer army in Libya. The U.S. Army had learned that fighting skilled *Wehrmacht* troops could produce many battlefield setbacks as well as high casualties. Battle casualties sustained by the Allied forces in the Algerian–French Moroccan campaign of November 8–11, 1942, were 1,469 killed, 887 wounded, and 52 missing. During the Tunisian campaign alone from November 12, 1942, to May 13, 1943, the Allies suffered 10,290 men killed, 38,688 wounded, and 21,363 missing. The Axis suffered nearly 200,000 battle casualties during the Tunisian campaign, of which 155,000 were German, along with approximately 275,000 Axis soldiers surrendering in what was dubbed "Tunisgrad," comparing the enemy capitulation in North Africa to the German Sixth Army yielding to the Russians at Stalingrad in February 1943.

In contradistinction to Eisenhower's humility, a huge victory parade was held through the streets of Tunis on May 20, 1943. Two American regiments marched behind a military band in new uniforms and with cleaned equipment. Following the Americans were the pipers of the Scots and Grenadier Guards leading Highland regiments, British infantry, Australians "diggers," Maoris, Sikhs, and Gurkhas. Perhaps the most colorful were the detachments of Spahis, Zouaves, Tirailleurs, Goums, and other colonial troops. Intriguingly, the French general Jacques-Philippe Leclerc and his men refused to march with the French units led by previous Vichy French generals Louise-Marie Koeltz (of the French XIX Corps) and Alphonse Juin, the French commander in Tunisia whom the Allies respected as a rebuilder of the French Army in North Africa. Leclerc's refusal to march also showcased the earlier factionalism between the two French military leaders of the day, Generals Charles Gaulle and Henri Giraud.

The cemeteries of all combatants dot the battlefield, with larger ones at lesser-known sites such as near Carthage, Takrouna, Enfidaville, Medjez, and Hammam Lif. The Italians eventually brought their fallen home for burial in their native soil. For many of the missing in action, only stone memorials with their names etched in commemorative aggregate exist.

The Northwest Africa campaign yielded an international Allied general staff that was integrated at both political and military levels. Cooperation between the British and Americans had survived some prickly tests both on and off the battlefield. Thus, if the Allied coalition could survive the hurdles posed by this initial campaign in Africa, optimistic anticipation was to remain for further operations in the Mediterranean, namely, on Sicily and the Italian mainland. Excellent battlefield and rear echelon commanders evolved, while scores of Allied officers at a variety of unit leadership levels were culled from combat command due to a lack of capable performance.

From a strategic standpoint the Allies now held a threat to the Axis positions in Sicily, Italy, the Balkans, Crete, and the Dodecanese Islands. They also held complete control of North Africa from the Atlantic coast to the Red Sea. Also, airfields along Africa's northern coast would enable long-range aerial penetration on bombing missions deep into the enemy's heartland.

On May 13, 1943, Gen. Sir Harold Alexander, commander of the 18th Army Group, proclaimed: "Today you stand as the conquerors and heroes of the North African shores. The world acknowledges your victory; history will acclaim your deeds. British, French, and American arms have swept from these lands the last of the German and Italian invaders."

Allied troops and Tunis residents celebrate the liberation of the city on May 8, 1943, as they parade down a tram track. The GI in the center is waving the French tricolor flag, and other members of the group include (from left to right) two other American soldiers, a French sailor, a British guardsman (wearing his customary stiff peaked hat), and three British tankers. NARA

American soldiers from the 135th Infantry Regiment of the U.S. 34th Division, who were selected to represent the United States for their valor at Hill 609 in Tunisia, march through Tunis during the victory parade of May 20, 1943, one week after the formal Axis surrender in Tunisia. They wore clean, new uniforms and had their weapons shouldered despite an afternoon temperature above ninety degrees. The crowds were several rows deep and shouted exhortations to the GIs from the balconies and rooftops overlooking the spectacle. NARA

The massed pipers and drummers of the Scots and Grenadier Guards regiments with the bagpipes skirling lead contingents of only the British First Army along the victory parade route, as a similar parade had been held for Montgomery's victorious Eighth Army after the fall of Tripoli in February 1943. NARA

A unit of French soldiers, with their typical long trench coats and helmets, march past the reviewing stand, having been led by Generals Juin and Koeltz. The size of the French contingent was unusually large—despite the absence of General de Gaulle's supporters who refused to march—probably to deliberately impress the local Arab population, some of whom desired independence from France. NARA

A French colonial Algerian contingent, wearing head turbans and sandals (or no shoes at all), is led by French officers in their white kepis. Both the officers and Algerian soldiers are wearing their customary white gandouras.
NARA

A French officer in his white kepi leads a contingent of Moroccan infantrymen, also referred to as Goumiers or Goums. The Moroccan soldiers, known for their fierce knife-fighting combat style, which often included collecting the ears of their vanquished enemy, march in the classic striped, woolen, loose-fitting hooded djellaba. Many are shouldering their long, antiquated desert rifles with attached bayonets. NARA

German prisoners are escorted to a stockade by an American military policeman. Of the almost 275,000 Axis prisoners taken, more than 100,000 were German. Many of the stockades teemed with prisoners of war (POWs) in the open until they were given small tents to shield them from the sun. Eventually some of these POWs would be transported in the empty hulls of Liberty ships back to the United States for internment for the duration of the war. NARA

A mass of Italian POWs smile at the camera. In the retreat from El Alamein and in Tunisia, many lacked motorized transport, with surrender being their only option as Allied mechanized forces moved forward. Although somewhat disputed, Allied records list the number of Italian POWs at the end of the Tunisian campaign as 135,000 to 170,000 troops and rear echelon soldiers. NARA

A temporary American cemetery at Les Andalouses, where U.S. soldiers fell during the initial combat after the Algerian landings from November 8–11, 1942. An Army honor guard fires a traditional salute after their recent burial. NARA

A U.S. Army chaplain supervises the burial of dead American soldiers killed in Tunisia. Their graves lie in soft sand, but the surrounding terrain, composed of scrub and cactus, was typical of the central Tunisia battlefield on which they died. NARA

Neat, well-ordered graves with markings of German soldiers who died in and around Tunis. Their ornate headstones bear their names and dates of birth and death. Many of the German deaths near Tunis were a result of the fanatical Nazi resistance and fierce counterattacks to deny the advancing Americans vital hills near the port city.
NARA

A well-kept gravesite of an Italian corporal from Bologna who died in February 1943 in fighting in Tunisia. This may have been more of a commemorative marker, since the Italians tried to reclaim their soldiers' remains for ultimate burial in Italian soil.
NARA

An Australian soldier pays his last respects to a fallen comrade, Cpl. John H. Edmonson of the 2/17th Infantry Battalion, at a well-kept Australian Imperial Force cemetery at Tobruk. He died during the initial days of the Tobruk siege and was awarded a posthumous Victoria Cross for his heroism on the battlefield. AWM

A Seaforth Highlander in the 51st Scottish Highland Division, wearing his traditional tam-o'-shanter with his Short Magazine Lee-Enfield (SMLE) rifle slung over his shoulder, pays his last respects to a fellow Scot who lies in a relatively fresh grave after perishing near Wadi Akarit and the Gabès Gap as Montgomery's Eighth Army pursued Rommel's *Panzer-Armee Afrika* in southern Tunisia after crossing the Libyan border. AUTHOR'S COLLECTION

A sketch of the Italian Fascist dictator, Benito Mussolini, lies trampled along a roadside accompanied by spent shell casings as Axis forces continue their retreat toward Bizerte in the spring of 1943. The Axis defeat was an incredible blow to Italy and rocked the prestige of the pretentious Mussolini. The Italians had lost their African colonies, along with any imperial delusions that they harbored, before the war in North Africa, Abyssinia, and Italian Somaliland began in earnest in December 1940. As Allied bombing of Italy intensified from newly constructed North African airfields, Mussolini and his Fascist Party seemed increasingly impotent in the eyes of ordinary Italians, who would soon begin their war-stricken ordeal on their own soil. USAMHI

Field Marshal Erwin Rommel with his *Deutsches Afrikakorps* officers shortly after the fall of Tobruk and the awarding of his field marshal baton in May 1942. His offensive against Montgomery with his German-Italian panzer army at Medenine was to be his last Tunisian battle, as he left North Africa permanently on March 9, 1943. After a long rest in Germany, Rommel commanded an army group in northern Italy in the autumn of 1943. After that he was sent by Hitler to supervise the construction of the Atlantic Wall prior to the Normandy invasion. In July 1944 he was injured following an RAF strafing raid, which forced his car to overturn in a ditch. Having been implicated in the July 1944 assassination attempt on Hitler, he was forced to commit suicide in the fall of 1944; however, he received a state funeral. NARA

Col. Gen. Hans-Jürgen von Arnim, commander in chief (C-in-C), *Panzer Armee Gruppe Afrika* (center), surrendering to Maj. Gen. Sir Bernard Freyberg, VC, C-in-C New Zealand Corps (left), on May 13, 1943. After his capture he remained a British POW until his release in July 1947. He died in Bad Wildungen, Germany, in September 1962. AWM

British and American leaders who had forged a victory with Operation Torch and the victory in Tunisia after the six-month campaign confer in North Africa in May 1943 for future operations. British prime minister Winston Churchill sits at the table with his trademark cigar (center). The trio behind him (from left to right) are Air Chief Marshal Arthur Tedder of the Royal Air Force; Adm. Andrew Cunningham, commander of the Mediterranean Fleet; and Field Marshal Sir Harold Alexander, C-in-C 18th Army Group. To the far left of Churchill are Anthony Eden, Britain's secretary for war, and Gen. Sir Alan Brooke (awarded field marshal rank in January 1944), chief, Imperial General Staff (CIGS). Seated to the right of Churchill are Generals George C. Marshall, U.S. Army chief of staff, and Dwight D. Eisenhower, supreme commander of Allied Forces. Standing to the far right is Gen. Bernard L. Montgomery, C-in-C British Eighth Army. NARA

Allied landing craft transports and landing craft infantry lie packed in at Bizerte harbor on July 2, 1943, in preparation for disembarking to join the convoy for Sicily with elements of the U.S. 3rd Infantry Division. NARA

Allied landing craft infantry LCI-122, part of the convoy steaming for the Sicilian invasion in July 1943. The conquest of North Africa gave the Allies control of the Mediterranean, with Sicily and the Italian mainland as planned targets to bring the war to Continental Europe. NARA

ACKNOWLEDGMENTS

I am grateful for the editorial guidance of David Reisch and the editorial assistance of Brittany Stoner and Ellen Urban at Stackpole Books, as well as to Philip Schwartzberg of Meridian Mapping in Minneapolis, Minnesota, for his cartographic expertise.

Archival images were obtained from the United States Military History Institute (USAMHI) in Carlisle, Pennsylvania; the Still Photo Section of the National Archives and Records Administration (NARA) in College Park, Maryland; the Library of Congress in Washington, DC; along with the digital archives of the Australian War Memorial (AWM). Some of the color photographs of weaponry were obtained from the Army Heritage Museum, United States Army Heritage Education Center, United States Army War College (AHM, USAHEC, USAWC) in Carlisle, Pennsylvania, and I would like to thank those curators for their assistance.

Finally, I would like to dedicate this book to the memories of all the men and women who served, were wounded, or gave their lives far from their homes during the Allied conquest of North Africa. These images and words are lasting reminders to us to never forget their sacrifices.

REFERENCES

Atkinson, R. *An Army at Dawn: The War in North Africa, 1942-1943*. New York: Henry Holt and Company, 2002.

Blumenson, M. *Kasserine Pass: Rommel's Climactic Battle for Tunisia*. New York: Cooper Square Press, 2000.

Breuer, W.B. *Operation Torch: The Allied Gamble to Invade North Africa*. New York: St. Martin's Press, 1985.

D'Este, C. *Patton: A Genius for War*. New York: Harper Collins, 1995.

Diamond, J. *Archibald Wavell*. Command. Oxford: Osprey Publishing, 2012.

Ford, K. *El Alamein 1942: The Turning of the Tide*. Campaign. Oxford: Osprey Publishing, 2005.

———. *The Mareth Line 1943: The End in Africa*. Campaign. Oxford: Osprey Publishing, 2012.

Howe, G.F. *Northwest Africa: Seizing the Initiative in the West*. Washington, D.C.: Department of the Army, 1978.

Jones, V. *Operation Torch: Anglo-American Invasion of North Africa*. New York: Ballantine Books, 1972.

Larrabee, E. *Commander in Chief: Franklin Delano Roosevelt, His Lieutenants, and Their War*. New York: Harper & Row, 1987.

Rolf, D. *The Bloody Road to Tunis: Destruction of the Axis Forces in North Africa, November 1942-May 1943*. London: Greenhill Books, 2001.

Rutherford, W. *Kasserine: Baptism of Fire*. New York: Ballantine Books, 1970.

Whiting, C. *Kasserine: The Battlefield Slaughter of American Troops by Rommel's Afrika Korps*. Briarcliff Manor, N.Y.: Stein and Day, 1984.

Zaloga, S.J. *Kasserine Pass 1943: Rommel's Last Victory*. Campaign. Oxford: Osprey Publishing, 2005.